T0090768

# DON'T FORGET YOUR KEYS
## *Each Key Holds the Power*
## *to Your Career Advancement*

By
Barbara B. Bergstrom

Order this book online at www.trafford.com
or email orders@trafford.com

Most Trafford titles are also available at major online book retailers.

© Copyright 2010 Barbara B. Bergstrom.
All rights reserved. No part of this publication may be reproduced, stored in a retrieval system, or transmitted, in any form or by any means, electronic, mechanical, photocopying, recording, or otherwise, without the written prior permission of the author.

Printed in Victoria, BC, Canada.

ISBN: 978-1-4269-3088-1 (sc)
ISBN: 978-1-4269-3027-0 (dj)
ISBN: 978-1-4269-3189-5 (e)

Library of Congress Control Number: 2010905175

*Our mission is to efficiently provide the world's finest, most comprehensive book publishing service, enabling every author to experience success. To find out how to publish your book, your way, and have it available worldwide, visit us online at www.trafford.com*

*Trafford rev. 4/28/2010*

Trafford
PUBLISHING®   www.trafford.com

North America & international
toll-free: 1 888 232 4444 (USA & Canada)
phone: 250 383 6864 ♦ fax: 812 355 4082

# *Introduction*

You don't know what you don't know, but *others* do. Once you know, you know who knows and who doesn't know. This could be carried on ad infinitum; however, consider yourself spared.

The *others,* the ones who "know," are ultimately responsible for your business success. The decision-makers are behind doors that are virtually locked, perhaps even bolted shut. Without the *keys* to unlock those doors, you can consider your future business success in dire jeopardy.

Some well-educated people, even those who have advanced degrees, believe their academic achievements are the *keys* to their ultimate success. Nothing could be further from the truth.

The fact is that no matter how technically trained, highly skilled, and heavily credentialed you are, the *keys* to your success are found in your soft skills, or how and what you communicate along with the image you project. Even when your voice is still, you are communicating volumes. To make certain that what is being communicated is what you want others to acknowledge as key-worthy is, in fact, a *key* in itself.

How frustrating it must be to have achieved so much and to hold long-term goals and aspirations only to become aware you don't know what it takes to open the doors to a successful future. The concepts of a great education, technical expertise, wit and a burning desire to succeed are fundamentally acceptable. The hard work of discovering how to move from vision to reality is quite difficult for some of us.

Which *keys* will make a difference? How do you acquire them? Why do doors open for some and not for everyone? Failure after several attempts to get through the door to decision-makers can become a blow to one's self-confidence. Shattered dreams of success will destroy the possibility of a bright career.

Without knowing where to turn for answers, even the most optimistic and assertive among us tend to become self-conscious, even embarrassed, as doors open all around for others while we fumble at the lock. Fortunately, the following pages are designed to bring some resolution to this quandary.

As you will soon discover, a primary factor in your success in opening the right doors is using the right *keys*. Using the *keys* proficiently becomes your professional presence. Knowing how to communicate your message and perform confidently, in any situation, are amazing confidence-building tools. They are at the core of your soft skills and *key* factors in determining how many doors ultimately will open for you.

As a corporate trainer, executive mentor, and nationally syndicated columnist, I have developed messages on the subject of professional presence that are resonating with executives throughout the world in many industry segments. These are the individuals who "know," and they also know who doesn't. These executives have professional presence and are often the ones waiting to extend, to you, the ultimate greeting as the door opens for you. They are the ones who will nurture a professional camaraderie as you carry your new standard.

I've had the opportunity to work closely with upper-level managers of many companies who have asked me to assess staffers and identify what would take them to the next level. The overwhelming shortcomings – seldom addressed in personnel reviews – are the differences between social and business etiquette. Although these two go hand in hand, they are quite different.

Most of us were raised learning social etiquette from our parents. It just doesn't always work in business. Professional presence is being familiar with and using the protocols necessary to conduct business globally in today's highly competitive environment. One must know how to make business introductions, network properly, and understand the nuances of navigating a business or diplomatic meal while also wearing the appropriate business attire. Each protocol or rule is a determinant in selecting the right *key*.

Consider carefully that the passages in this book reflect not only my experience, but also that of those active in the decision-making process. The management hierarchy, the human resource door guards or sentinels, and the executive recruiters are the ones who will evaluate your potential.

The bottom line is that you and your peers are being assessed on factors far beyond your technical abilities, personality or past performance. To get through certain doors, the most coveted ones, you must embrace and embody a more powerful quality that defines your personal presence. That quality is civility, a century-old practice founded on respect for yourself and others. It is the *key* that will set you apart from your competition.

After you read the offerings and guidelines in this book, you will know and understand what others don't. You will be able to reach your true potential in the competitive global battle for talent. Leaders seek out, select and promote those who "know."

You will now have the *keys*. Don't leave home without them!

# A Special Note

Greetings to those of you who have the desire to do business globally, especially in the United States, and empower yourselves with a contemporary professional presence.

With the help of this book and the information it contains, you will learn the secrets and cross-cultural sensitivities you must possess to become a world-class business professional. You will be given the keys and business knowledge necessary to avoid offending when this was not your intent. You will appear to everyone as a professional by your words, your attire, and your manner at meals and in meetings – and by practicing the helpful information on the following pages.

This book is intended for the person who wishes to do business in the United States as well as in other countries and to give you the keys to know what others do not. To understand the American thought process, the following information will serve you well.

U.S. society is composed of people from many social, cultural, ethnic, religious and national backgrounds with different economics and philosophies of life.

We consider ourselves individuals, and individual rights are important to us. Americans have strong family ties and an honest respect for other people, and they insist on human equality.

Honesty and directness are more important than "saving face," and we may bluntly bring up topics that to others may seem embarrassing, controversial or offensive. Generally informed, we are respectful and even sentimental about tradition but not social ritual.

Although competitive because we place high value on achievement, we also have a good sense of "teamwork," working with others to achieve a goal.

We are uncomfortable with long periods of silence except in our personal surroundings with family. Most of us will say almost anything in social or business settings because it is better than silence.

We are friendly, smile often and ask a lot of questions. No impertinence is intended as the questions come from a genuine interest. You are encouraged to ask questions. Don't hesitate, because as Americans, we are open and eager to explain or share information.

Punctuality is valued because we are time-conscious. We keep appointment calendars and fill our days doing many things with energy because we live in a highly active society. Others may think we are rushing, which is not the case at all.

Many Americans take their health seriously, exercise frequently and have become anti-smoking advocates. Smoking is not permitted in government and office buildings, airports, schools, hospitals and some restaurants.

In keeping with our attitude about the importance of time, business executives will generally want to get right down to business. To them, time is money and should not be wasted on formalities and lengthy discussions. Being decisive and efficient are valued qualities, while indecision is taken as a sign of poor management. In most cases, be assured, however, that you will be treated fairly and openly and given enough time to express yourself.

It is an advantage to all doing business internationally that the multicultural person should recognize, accept and appreciate our differences in culture, religion and national heritage. We must be willing to accept, appreciate and respect our basic unity as human beings.

Finally, the American business person relies on the keys of respect, trust, appreciation and professional presence. If you want to do business in the United States, *don't forget your keys.*

# *Dedication*

To: My Heavenly Father, my loving family and friends.

To: All those who have crossed my path at one time
or another and given me "the keys."

To: All the working warriors seeking a professional presence
in practice fields and in business arenas
nationally and internationally:
"Don't Forget Your Keys."

I thank you all.

Barbara

# Contents

# PROFESSIONALISM

# The Power of Professionalism

We yearn for professional presence in all that we do but truthfully a small percentage of the millions who conduct business daily are truly professional.

Although many amateurs look like professionals in the way they dress and groom themselves, the outward appearance disguises the amateur inside.

Amateurs have a tendency to focus on themselves. Often you will hear them use the pronouns "I" or "me," as a prefix, in the center of most of their communication pattern. The professionals will use "We." They know that they seldom do things single-handedly in business. The amateur is often branded as an egocentric.

Amateurs are concerned about discounts, price and what's in it for them. Often they haggle over who receives the most attention or the biggest slice of the pie. Talking to the client or prospect about how much they can provide or do for them is another signal that an amateur is at work.

A professional listens to the needs of the prospect then goes about filling those needs. Sensitivity to what drives the need becomes a factor. The professional takes measures to assure the need is fulfilled to the benefit of the customer not themselves. Professionals will follow-up, while amateurs leave loose ends untied. Instead of worrying about a piece of the pie, professionals create more and bigger pies.

Professionalism creates a tremendous power because people want to do business with those who are committed to excellence. In turn, excellence creates more business.

It is not good enough these days to just put in a hard days work. You must do what ever it is you do better than your competition to even be considered professional. The basic virtues of respect, dignity, courtesy, honesty and trust are tools needed to be found in the professional's tool box. Professionals go out of their way to assure every client feels their focus and also feels appreciated.

Generally, the professionals love what they do and they continually develop skills and knowledge about their products and services. This enables them to do what they do better than anyone else.

Don't confuse profession with occupation. An occupation is a job – a job that unfortunately so many don't want to be doing in the first place. You've heard the expression, I'm sure, "What I really wanted to do or be in my life was ..."

It is virtually impossible to become a true professional if you really don't even like what you're doing. It is sad but so many people are just putting in their time, doing at best, the least that is expected. Others are dedicated to working very hard, day in and day out, doing something they hate. Most often their career interests actually lie somewhere else hidden in their dreams.

Becoming skilled professionals, who are in demand and prized by industry leaders, doesn't just happen. They must take a keen interest in their career and be producers – make bigger pies, be disciplined and show respect to others at all times. In addition, they must practice diplomacy, be considerate, soft-spoken yet firm and really like people. They must be encouraging, free with praise of others, dress appropriately and do their homework. The professional may also have a few other qualities, which aren't totally without merit, often found in Saints.

Finally, professionals look for and seem to see the invisible and accomplish the impossible. When the power of professionalism is generated, success is a given.

# Improving Yourself

What are you doing to improve yourself? What makes you better today than you were yesterday or a month ago? Ah ha, you might answer, "Finding my keys in this book."

I certainly don't mean to buy your ticket for a guilt trip, but I do want to challenge your comfort zone just a bit.

Sometimes we all have a tendency to slack off or perhaps sit back and rest on our laurels. We make choices all day long, every day of the week and unfortunately, often we just choose not to grow. We've done it. We've been there and we become very comfortable with our routine. We also become complacent.

Are you really as successful as you would like to be? Are you going through the motions or are you growing with your motions?

Successful people are growing all the time. By doing the same, you broaden your horizons by exercising your mind and your body, reading, listening, viewing and sometimes even letting go. Yes, letting go of yesterday's mindset and also some of the bad habits collected along your career path.

Often, we think we do a lot but nothing really seems to get done. We even do some of the same things over and over again. Boredom sets in and frustration follows because we confuse activity with accomplishment.

Something as simple and useful as being current with what is acceptable conduct, in the business arena, will contribute to your well-being and positively affect those around you. Social etiquette and business etiquette are similar but in certain areas and under professional guidelines are really quite different. You must know the difference to make a difference. Do you know the difference or are you using today what your mother taught you many years ago? We have some personal mountains to climb and positive action is necessary to encourage growth. For example, business etiquette requires you to stop transferring blame. Your performance is your responsibility. Own it! You choose your behavior and the way you treat others therefore you also choose the consequences.

I can't remember who it was that pointed out to me that I have actually chosen to be a tad more than ten pounds overweight. The reason I'm tipping the scales on the high side is because I have never sat down and accidentally eaten anything! I did it. I chose to eat it today and wear it tomorrow. I can't blame anyone else, because it was no ones choice but mine. I own it.

Along the same line of thinking if I choose to remain stagnant in my career, without putting forth effort into improving myself, it stands to reason that I have also chosen to decrease my income.

Just think about it. If you are going to change your status you must improve your performance. You must motivate yourself. No one can do it for you. No matter how many self help books you read, or motivational speakers you hear, it all comes down to you doing it! Your motivation must come from within yourself based on your personal daily choices.

When you take responsibility and motivate yourself, you become an inner-directed employee. In today's competitive business arena independent mentally flexible employees have raised the bar. Even one size fits all work schedules are doomed. More work is done away from the office and at home thanks to all the technology we have at our finger-tips today. Realtors tell me the four bedroom house is no longer a four bedroom home. It is three bedrooms and an office. The typical three-bedroom, two-bath house or condo is now two bedrooms, two baths and an office.

I have a plaque in my office, within my direct line of sight. I can't miss it. It reads, "If it's going to be, it's up to me." It reminds me daily to stop moaning and start moving. I must make things happen. It has taught me that the choices I make, affect not only me, but all those with whom I come in contact. How I treat people, talk, smile, respond, respect them and consider them, in all that I do, is up to me. If I don't choose to manage myself and my own attitude, how can I ever lead anyone else?

Taking action liberates your energy and is a great builder of confidence. Sometimes you procrastinate and don't fulfill tasks you know need to be completed. You unfortunately develop leaks in your energy reservoir and fatigue saps your time and creativity. Procrastination and blame will literally paralyze your productivity.

Now is the time to renew your determination and your desire to be all that you can be. Show respect and appreciate your opportunities. Let excuses be a part of your past – the part you let go. Begin each day by saying to yourself. "If it's going to be, it's up to me!"

# *Adversity*

If you boil water in three pans, add carrots to the first, eggs to the second and coffee to the third, this set of simple actions teaches us something about facing adversity.

The carrots go into the water hard but come out soft and weak. The eggs go into the water fragile but come out hardened. The coffee changes the water to something better.

As you face life will you become soft and give up, become hard or will you transform adversity into triumph? What will you bring to the table in your own life?

Liberace, the famed pianist, said "Nobody will believe in you unless you believe in yourself."

Sometimes we do things that we really don't believe in. When this happens, we tend to lose sight of who we truly are. Only you can be yourself. No one else is qualified for the job. Often we try so hard to be perfect when we really should work the hardest at being ourselves. We must learn to deal with adversity and how to overcome it in our own way.

Adversity is thrust upon us in different measures and how we choose to handle it affects our world.

For some adversity comes into our life like an ever-changing kaleidoscope and changes the pattern we laid out for our life. Some others are born into adversity and must learn survival tactics. When adversity is conquered, the skills learned, in the doing, are the golden treasures of life's experience.

The foundation of all working relationships, business and personal, begins with your own self-esteem. We all experience set backs and when you meet adversity or difficulties head-on you either alter the difficulties or you must alter yourself to meet them.

I believe whole heartily in this quote from Brian Tracey, "Develop an attitude of gratitude, and give thanks for everything that happens to you knowing that every step forward is a step toward achieving something bigger and better than your current situation."

Are you the carrot who has become soft? Do you whine and complain while asking, why me? Do you dig down deep into yourself for the strength and ability to change the adversity thrust upon you?

The strength is there but you must go after it, use it and make the choices necessary to effect change. Your fellow employees or business associates can't do it for you. In fact, they will probably leave you to your own devices and give their attention and sympathy to others they feel really needs it leaving you to wallow in your own pity pot.

Are you the egg who has become hard, dictatorial and domineering? Do you tell others what to do instead of asking them? Is the working environment you have created pleasant, cohesive and team-oriented? Is there a feeling of harmony? Ask yourself if you are taking out your frustration and disappointment on others rather than looking inward into yourself for change.

Finally, are you that person who meets the challenge head-on and alters yourself? The one who uses adversity as an opportunity to make something better of yourself, your surroundings, your business and your relationships?

Don't forget, when it begins to hurt, you will change. You hold the key! You have the power and adversity has given you the motivation for change.

Great leaders have all dealt with adversity at one time or another, in one form or another, in different degrees. When adversity knocks, recognize it as the tool you need to achieve the greatest success in your chosen field – perhaps in your life. Embrace it! Become a leader! You hold the key!

# Women and the Glass Ceiling

Respect for women prior to the 1970s required a man to practically jump through hoops to prove he was gallant. Chivalry demanded that he had to stand up when a woman entered a room, was being seated at a table or when she excused herself and left the table. He had to carry her packages, hold her coat, open all doors, including the car door and unfortunately, light her cigarettes.

When dining out, a woman would tell her escort what she wanted to order for dinner and he would, in turn, tell the waitperson. A woman didn't talk to the wait staff unless she was dining with another woman and the interaction couldn't be avoided.

A woman wasn't allowed in the Boardroom except to pour coffee, fill water glasses or take dictation. Business wasn't discussed in front of her because it was thought that she wouldn't understand.

Obviously, she did understand! Women have become a moving force in business and government today throughout the world. They have made many changes in the business etiquette protocols from the past to the present. Today, a man doesn't have to wait for a woman to extend her hand for a handshake. The first person to extend the hand has the advantage.

Internationally, where men would not even touch women much less shake their hands, customs have also changed. In the Muslim religion, men do not shake a woman's hand but just as in Thailand and other parts of the world, it is understood and permissible for business people to shake hands. Yes, even if one of the parties is a woman.

The rules of the game of business have definitely changed; however, respect remains steadfast no matter the culture. In some countries where a hug and kiss on each cheek is the custom, the handshake most always precedes this form of welcome.

Along the same line of gender neutral customs in the United States, the first person to reach the door opens it as a common gesture of courtesy.

Some men have a difficult time understanding their masculinity is not diminished when a woman opens the door. She is just being polite because she got there first. A man would do the same for another man as an act of courtesy.

In business, women are or should be treated as equals with men and most often are, however, they still have a long way to go to correct some inadequacies and level the playing field. This holds true especially in the area of salaries.

It is a joy to see and an inspiration for women to appreciate that the time is NOW and the place is HERE. Women need to reject intimidation and innuendo. Their ambition must not be depressed. Sometimes women shoot themselves in the foot by taking the past inequities with them as they try to move forward.

Differences between men and women are obvious in meetings. Men say what they mean to say and women very often begin with, "May I make a comment?" or "May I offer a suggestion?" This shows the lack of confidence they bring into the business arena from the social etiquette they were taught as young ladies. No way is a man going to ask permission and women in the non-gender competitive business world should just say what they have to say.

Women today must also not be afraid to say "no" when they are overloaded and have reached their limit. Women were taught to please and often feel as though their job is in jeopardy if they can not do all and be all to their male supervisors. Failure is a heavy hammer they actually impose on themselves.

Women need to accept responsibility and feel empowered. They should never make excuses because the focus is switched and the sight of the original goal is lost.

Women have come a long way in the United States and now hold powerful positions as CEO's of mega companies as well as high level government positions. But this is the exception in many other countries even though we are very familiar with the names of a few outstanding women in high offices.

The greatest numbers of women decision makers outside of the United States are from Western Europeans countries. England's former Prime

Minister, Margaret Thatcher, is one of the most well-known and admired leaders throughout the world.

The American business woman has become a role-model for working women in the Middle East. The Arabs don't feel comfortable doing business with women but they certainly are aware of the U.S. women's business achievements. In Japan and China, women are increasingly on the business scene.

We are fortunate that, in these United States, our business customs have changed consistently. Contemporary men are still gallant in the social environment and respect is alive and well socially and in business even though some people wonder where it is hiding. While our business climate dictates status and position are the big factors, gender is not and age does not take precedent. I like that!

It is true that many businesses today are recognizing the need for diversity on their Boards of Directors. Women are still noticeably under-represented. The majority of the persons seated currently on corporate boards is male, white and largely share the same backgrounds, views, interests and circles of influence.

It is a given that monolithic backgrounds foster monolithic thinking. When companies bring together a diversity of people, ideas flow and innovation emerges. Some women have crashed through the glass ceiling but unfortunately the numbers are really not that impressive. On foreign boards Scandinavia takes the lead in the number of women with board seats due to proactive policies and quotas. The rest of Europe lags behind but an interesting show of diversity comes to light as many men seated on European boards are of a different nationality than their company.

Since my chosen career is relative to thoughtful consideration of others, or the "nice business," my experience tells me that women are generally pre-conditioned and seen as not ambitious. Even though they may be quite the opposite, they have a tendency to play down their accomplishments and fail to push for their raises and promotions. In their book *Women Don't Ask: Negotiation and the Gender Divide,* Linda Babcock and Sandra Caschever tell us girls are taught to be "communal," to make relationships a priority and to focus on the needs of others instead of their own.

Today, women in the corporate community must actively seek potential opportunities to serve on boards. Just as Prince Charming is not going to come and knock on the door without knowing his princess even exists, women cannot sit back and expect board appointments to just come their way. When women take charge of their future, take credit for their accomplishments, build connections and seek opportunities, the fruits of their labor will make an impression on the decision makers.

Sports were always a major part of the lives of my three sons and my daughter. Having three older brothers, the girl in the family learned how to throw a spiral football and received her college scholarship by playing basketball. Competition was eaten and digested in my household.

With sports comes a willingness to talk about accomplishments. Boys and some girls learn, at an early age, to talk about winning and being first in a race, ballgame or being the conference champions. In business, the idea of competition is innate with men. They talk about accomplishments to others – their clients, co-workers and yes, to their boss.

Women, with few exceptions, get their recognition or encouragement for being discreet, sociable, attractive, quiet and non-competitive. They also get overlooked for senior executive positions. It really is unusual for many women to applaud their own accomplishments and embrace self-promotion. It is sad but must be said that many women are passed over or passed by for advancement due to their own lack of awareness and action. Men understand the importance of self-promotion while women often become their own worst enemy.

What does all this have to do with executive etiquette? I have mentioned several times that business etiquette and social etiquette, though similar in come respects, are actually quite different. In business age and gender should not be recognized. Women need to speak up. There is some truth to the question, "Why can't a woman be more like a man?" Men speak up and do it naturally.

In a meeting, for example, if a woman has an idea or wants to express herself, often she will ask permission to speak or even begin with an apology before saying what she has to say. Men would never do that. If men have something to say, they say it.

This is not rude behavior on the men's part; it is "get to the point" business behavior. Women are so fearful of being over-bearing or too aggressive often they sit back and hope to be noticed and appreciated. Interruption is unacceptable but so is being reticent. Brain-storming sessions are a necessity in meetings and so are getting their ideas on the table. It is important for them to be heard if they are women who want to be noticed and whose opinions and ideas are valued.

I don't mean to suggest or encourage an "in your face" demeanor which automatically will reduce any chance for advancement. Boasting and bragging are also unacceptable. Women need to talk to the right people about their work and accomplishments and how they got the job done. They need to ask for some face time with the boss and keep their sights on where they want to be this time next year. They must set goals and focus on doing whatever they do better than anyone else does it. That is what competition in the business arena is all about: playing the game fairly, knowing the rules and playing better than the competition.

If women can't play better right now then they must work, study and grow until they can. When they hit the mark, they should let everyone know – especially those in whose hands lie career advancement and promotions to the boardroom. The glass ceiling has been cracked by many women in these Unites States, which shows it can and is being done. The numbers will increase as women become more confident and less fearful about taking responsibilities in roles they have thought they never could do. Instead of thinking they can't do something, they should try it – they may even like it. When women take charge of their own lives and their future in the business community, they will find the glass ceiling is much lower than imagined. It is not mission impossible – it is mission critical for women to take more responsibility and continue to strive for equal pay. It is very possible for women today to achieve their desired level of success and raise the numbers of board appointments. They hold the key to their own level of success.

If you are a woman, **just do it!**

# The Ultimate Greeting

Attending lunches and meetings, spreading greetings, net-working and building relationships are necessities for us if we are to succeed in our chosen fields. I have noticed as I attend many of these touch point events that the message still hasn't been received by many active business persons regarding the ultimate greeting, the correct business handshake.

For those who don't yet know what others do, the handshake is one of the first calls for judgment. The proper business handshake speaks volumes about you, your confidence level and professional presence.

To say that one is non-judgmental is a misnomer. Of course a judgment is made when you experience a wimpy limp-fish handshake. If the handshake is bone-crushing, a judgment is also made instantly, along with a silent "ouch." To judge someone by certain criteria, the handshake being one of these criteria, is a natural re-action, therefore, it is critical to get each of our important first impression opportunities right the first time.

Many people think the business handshake is easy. They have seen it done and know what to do. Just stick your hand out and shake the other person's hand. Add a "good ol' boy" slap on the back and you're seen as open and friendly. What's the big deal? Who needs lessons? Obviously, those many people do. This manner of greeting is improper in business and is downright offensive in the global market.

Unfortunately, some women were taught to shake hands by their well-intentioned mothers, who were not in business but were dedicated homemakers. Some women were not taught how to shake hands, they just watched and "picked it up." Only a few fathers taught their daughters the business handshake, while most Dads taught their sons or the young men learned while serving in the military.

The mothers often taught daughters the finger-tip handshake and/or the wimpy handshake that "ladies" were supposed to use. Ladies, I can guarantee that doesn't work in today's non-gender business arena. If you present your hand in this manner, you have announced immediately that you are not the professional you envision yourself to be.

In the contemporary business community, the first person to extend their hand has the advantage. Men, do not wait for a woman to extend her hand before you extend yours. That custom went out of style years ago, along with the leisure suit.

The correct business handshake is used by men and women and is grip to grip or web to web. Try to avoid shaking the fingers and shake hands from the elbow not the wrist. Don't stand fixed to the floor but step forward into a handshake.

Today it is important for everyone to stand for a handshake and an introduction, at all times. The only exception for not standing for a handshake would be if one has a disability and cannot stand or is seated tightly at a table for ten which should be set for eight. An apology for not standing shows that you do know the correct protocol however.

To not stand is very noticeable, in the professional arena, and is a basic lack of courtesy to the person being greeted or the one being introduced. There are so many women in business today that the social custom of women remaining seated is now unacceptable in business and at social events as well.

Avoid the hand-over-hand or gloved handshake which is not appropriate in business. This is a condolence handshake and is better used at funerals and wakes or when consoling someone. And, try to avoid touching the other person, such as grabbing the arm or putting your arm around their shoulder. These are friendly gestures which should be reserved for a social greeting not a business meeting.

Shake hands with one or two pumps and then let go. Patting the hand is condescending and holding on too long is irritating and the motives for holding on to the hand too long may be questionable.

Never carry anything in your right hand and always be ready for a handshake even when you are walking down the street. You may meet an all important person coming your way and you don't want to fumble as you switch items from your right hand to your left. This takes a little practice as we have a tendency to carry things in our right hand most of the time, if we are right handed. A good place to practice is in the corridor of your office building. You meet and greet customers or clients often right there.

You should always shake hands when entering a room and greeting those you already know and meeting those you don't. The handshake is also given when leaving, consoling, congratulating, thanking, hosting and being introduced. When you are a speaker you shake hands with the introducer when you arrive at the lectern and again after your presentation as you return control of the lectern to the introducer and leave the podium.

Keep your right hand dry. That drink with the condensation on the glass is in your left hand-right? You know the feeling – your hand is wet and you wipe it on your trousers or skirt before you shake hands and say "excuse me." You know that's true and some of you have done it.

Women, when in a restaurant, don't carry a drink at all. Let the waitperson or your male escorts carry your drink to the table for you. A drink in your hand does nothing of value for your appearance.

If you are going to attend an event where you will be shaking many hands for hours, it is wise for men or women to avoid wearing a ring on the right hand. You could be in pain as time goes on and your ring finger may also begin to swell.

When clammy hands are a problem, use a deodorant on them 24 hours before the event. It really helps. Also, carry a small bottle of antiseptic wash to occasionally and discreetly dot on the palms of your hands. It will certainly keep you healthy and also remove the scent of a powerful perfume or cologne worn by some uninformed women and yes, some men too.

Shake hands with persons with disabilities. If the right hand is incapacitated, shake the left. If the person is paraplegic touch their shoulder.

Try to avoid shaking hands across a desk, table or another person. It puts a barrier between you. Make the effort to approach the person you are greeting and don't forget direct eye contact. If someone comes into your office, stand up and come around the desk to greet him and shake hands.

Finally, there is no huggy-bear, kissie-face in business. Avoid gestures of affection. If someone hugs you, don't push them away. This is not good form. Many people, especially those from the romance countries, are very demonstrative and hugging is a custom of their culture. You don't want to offend. You should try to avoid initiating the hug in business however, to keep things on a professional not personal level. Respond politely to a hug and consider the intent of the giver.

It is no wonder we sometimes become confused on this issue as Leo Buscaglia, PhD. of U.S.C., the "love doctor," before he passed on, taught us to hug anyone and everyone regularly and often. He did most of his teaching in California, which says a lot in itself. I assure you that business protocol, throughout the world, requires a tad more restraint for the professional business executive and the ultimate greeting, the correct business handshake, is a form of language everyone understands throughout the world.

# A Rose is a Rose

"A rose by any other name would smell as sweet," William Shakespeare wrote. You can bet he wasn't talking about courtesy titles used in business.

Is it Mr., Mrs., Miss or Ms.? What happened to the social traditions of calling a young boy Master?

The long-standing practice of using courtesy titles when speaking to customers or in business introductions even professionally seems to be confusing, fading or even lost altogether.

Today informality seems to have taken over by those who are not familiar with the protocols of business etiquette or are misguided.

Etiquette, in the business arena, is quite different and has certain practices that differ from those we learned in our social training. Not knowing the differences can lead to negative opinions about our qualifications. Many things said innocently or thought to be warm and friendly are actually insulting to some and come across as offensive to others.

When conducting business, your customers and clients remember each touch point. You should always make doing business with you an unforgettable pleasurable experience based on respect.

For example, when you address an envelope for business or personal correspondence, always use the honorifics Mr., Ms., Mrs., Miss or Doctor (Dr.). Failure to do so implies you don't care or don't know. Ms. is the correct title when speaking to or introducing a woman in the business arena regardless of what she chooses to call herself in her private life.

First-name droppers usually are young or have a casual personality. No slight is intended even though it may seem likely. Usually they will defend their informality or casual language due to a long-term business relationship or a preference stated by the customer. Corporate culture also plays a part. For example, if one is selling trucks the attitude is a tad less formal than when selling luxury automobiles. Older clients tend to expect a courtesy title. However, younger or older, a client or customer should never be called by the first name unless permission do to so has been given.

Most of us are naturally drawn to a person who is cheerful. However, try to eliminate the words "Hi" and "Hello." This may sound unusual, but just think about it. Any 18-month-old child can say "Hi." Isn't that cute? The greeting "Hello" is too abrupt and never enough. "Yo" is out of the question. I actually had a local bank president answer "Yo" when I called him. He unfortunately assumed incorrectly that I was someone else. Big mistake!!!!!

Always answer your phone calls professionally every time. You just never know. The call could be from a customer or client who could represent your entire budget for the coming year.

You might try glancing at the clock before picking up the receiver, to check the time of day. Answer with a smile and "Good Morning," "Good Afternoon," or "Greetings" and give your name.

It seems some people just abhor the use of honorifics or courtesy titles. Others say it makes them feel elderly or old-fashioned. The one thing these same people have ignored is the fact that in business it's not about them or what they like or don't like personally. It is all about the customers and their perception. Your success depends on these customers and clients. They represent your paycheck and it's all about the way they feel about you and their desire to buy your product or service.

People like to do business where they are known, appreciated and respected. Good manners are not old-fashioned and never go out of style. Is it really so difficult to say "Good Morning, Mr. Brown?" The response just may be the permission, "Please call me Joe." And, by the way, Master is very seldom used in business until the young boy becomes an adult and is respectfully referred to as Mister Brown.

Don't forget, calling a person by his or her name has a comforting ring to it. It is key because people love to hear their own name – it's beautiful and so is your smile!

# Respect

In every city and village the outcry is the same, "Where did it go - we want it back." The desire for etiquette consciousness is infiltrating the core values of our people everywhere. There is an awakening to the thoughtfulness, consideration and respect that reflect the words and actions of our heritage.

Unlike the previous generation, today, we actually pay to attend movies where our families, friends and most of all, our children, are pummeled with words and story lines that socially do not raise our standards, but reverse the trend for excellence in all that we do. Certainly, how you choose to spend your money is up to you but don't forget the choices you make have an effect on all those with whom you come in contact.

Exposing yourself and members of your family to words and actions which under normal circumstances, would be totally unacceptable, definitely has an influence on your language, attitude and what is known as acceptable conduct. You may counter with the fact that foul language, disgusting behavior, immorality and violence are part of life today and film makers are bringing forth realism. I remind you that diarrhea, regurgitation and your local garbage dump are also facts of life but I don't see a box office selling tickets for you to watch them. The point is that as our society becomes numbed to the unacceptable, we lower our personal standards and the crude and disgusting have a tendency to become commonplace in our behavior. If you find that you are allowing yourself to slide into that zone, an attitude adjustment is in order. Your career is at stake and your life will be affected negatively. I suggest you rethink your options and your choices.

In the competitive business arena, like it or not, management equates good manners with competence and bad manners with incompetence. A vital component to business success is not only being familiar with the rules or protocols of the game, but also playing by those rules. No matter what your title, foul language and rude behavior is unacceptable in the game of business anywhere, at any time. The rules are merely a part of the game, but without them, playing the game properly and winning are out of the question.

You may be just as technically trained as your competition, but to become a leader, you must have self-confidence. To win in the game of business, you must also have excellent communication and presentation skills, consideration and a healthy dose of respect for yourself and for those with whom you come in contact. You need to do whatever it is you do even better than your competition. By putting aside the mundane and concentrating on your professional presence you can "outclass" your competition and create the desire for customers and clients to want to do business with you because they are welcomed, known, appreciated and most of all, RESPECTED!

# *Honesty*

Honesty is an absolute and the cornerstone of any relationship. Unfortunately, we live in a world filled with deception. We profess to exercise correct behavior, respect and civility in business, however, ethics and honesty need to be addressed, due to the rampant abuse of our honor system. We can all wish that we could have faith and trust in those with whom we do business but wishing doesn't make it so.

The U.S. President Abraham Lincoln asked the question, "How many legs would a sheep have if he called his tail a leg?" The answer is four. Calling it something doesn't make it a fact. Believing everything we are told, in business, makes us naïve if not totally gullible, mislead and disillusioned.

Is it lying when we make a statement we believe to be true and later, due to changing circumstances, we must change our position? Is it lying when we break a promise? Is it lying when we deliberately mislead? Is it lying when we embellish or when we selectively omit facts relevant to employment? Or, are these little white lies acceptable and don't really count?

When one applies for a job, the resume is created and presented to the hiring entity. We believe the educational background and experience, as listed, are the initial announcements of a person's character, intent and qualifications as an accurate presentation of the facts.

Unfortunately, we have slipped so far down the list of ethical behavioral standards that today companies spend much more time and money on background checks and verification of academic records than ever before.

Career Builders.com conducted a survey recently which found over half of the Human Resource Managers surveyed said they flagged lies on applicants' resumes. Needless to say 93% of those who lied were not hired.

Sometimes it takes years for the falsehoods to rise to the surface. In some cases, it only takes minutes. In the case of Notre Dame Football Coach George O'Leary, it took just five days for him to resign. It took eleven years for Dave Edmonson, the CEO of Radio Shack, to be found out, in 2006, when he then resigned.

Academic discrepancies are the most common misrepresentation on resumes but dishonesty raises its ugly head in many major actions. Stealing, embezzlement, forging, counterfeiting, fraud are all obviously illegal and punishable to the full extent of the law.

The question today is, can you be trusted?

If you have an expense account, do you spend lavishly? Whose money is it? The money you spend belongs to the company, but the spending attitude is completely yours. Would you spend your own money lavishly, foolishly or wastefully? Certainly not! Be trustworthy and don't pad your expense account. You will not fool anyone and you will call attention to your level of dishonesty.

If you have a business outside of your primary income-producing employment, keep it outside of your primary employment. Do not bring catalogs, advertising materials, and cosmetic samples or vitamin supplements into your work environment. Doing so places pressure on your fellow workers to buy and it conflicts with your job responsibilities which are to the company who hired you and pays you to represent it, not your moonlighting income production.

Do you just "take a few" office supplies home with you? Perhaps product samples the company will "never miss." How often do you call in sick and go to a ballgame or take a Friday or Monday off and someone else has to cover for you and do your work?

Gossip? Some employees actually start rumors that have no foundation of truth, just to put doubt in the minds of management regarding promotion. Dishonesty is dishonesty to any degree.

What you do here, what you see here, what you hear here, let it stay here. When you discuss the business plans or intimacies concerning the company, you may just be giving away the store!

Unless you are the owner of the store or business, remember it is not yours to give away. Even discussing private business with your family over the dinner table, may prove to be costly. Respect company confidentiality.

Most companies do not object to an infrequent personal phone call, if it is short in duration. Never put anything in an e-mail you don't want saved to a master file or spend time, which is valuable, on off color jokes, non-essential trivia and personal messages.

Don't forget you are paid for time worked, not spent on personal phone calls, letters, or complaints about management and colleagues. Address your sister's birthday card on your lunch break.

These examples may sound like nit-picking minor offenses to some however, remember Abraham Lincoln's quote—calling it something else doesn't change it. Dishonesty runs rampant. Along your career path your reputation needs to remain stellar. Your reputation is a key.

Character, self-image and honesty, along with traditional values, surely make a difference in the business community. Taking this a step further, when parents instill good character traits in their children and are role models in actions, as well as words, we get back to the basic standards of right and wrong. Not only will the business community benefit but also the future of our country.

# Assumptions

One of the most dangerous words, one that often leads to disaster in business today, is "assumption."

Management cannot assume everyone is in agreement or even understands the message being conveyed. One cannot assume to know if a certain party is guilty of an offense or an error without obtaining all the facts. Using gut feelings or making assumptions based on reputation, poor performance, innuendo, expectations, hearsay or various other intangible measurements are tantamount to falling off a cliff.

If you are in a position to make a presentation, for example, don't presume your audience shares your beliefs. You could possibly offend. I know from experience as I found myself doing just that.

I was speaking to a group of M.B.A. students about the rules of the game of business and used the game of basketball as a metaphor. Some audience members were offended because I assumed most young students, male or female, know how to play basketball.

The valuable lesson I learned about assumption was to avoid casting a wide net. A much better way to use the metaphor would have been, "consider the game of basketball" rather than assume as students they know how to play the game.

Very often assumptions are formed about a speaker based on reputation, experiences or appearances even before a word is uttered. Are those assumptions correct? Let's turn the tables. Do you, as a speaker or presenter, form opinions about your audience for the very same reasons or perhaps what you expect them to be like based on pre-conceived notions or assumptions?

Dale Carnegie, who knew how to win friends and influence people said, "You are not dealing with creatures of logic, but with creatures of emotion, creatures bristling with prejudice and motivated by pride and vanity."

Be inclusive rather than exclusive while making those you address or work with feel you are in the same boat. Respect for you grows if you are generous with your praise. It is difficult to dislike someone who makes you feel well-liked and appreciated. Make certain your acknowledgements are sincere to avoid being seen as condescending or phony either on the platform or in the office. You will have the attention of those around you and they will be happy to be in your boat paddling with you, not against you.

One may assume an executive or someone, whose credentials are admired, is the epitome of good taste. That picture or assumption is often shattered when the person being admired opens his mouth.

Seafarers often use much better language than is heard today in numerous posh business offices. Many, especially young, M.B.A. recipients think nothing of using foul language in everyday conversation. They think it is all right but it is not perfectly all right. Word pollution tarnishes the image of the user and the companies they represent.

If we conduct meetings, as the leaders, we assume, everyone is in attendance to learn, participate or if nothing else, to listen. Body language betrays the attendees who are not the least bit interested. In business, attitude is everything. A sure-fire gauge for revealing a less than positive attitude is body language. It will either be pleasant, attentive and polite or negative, bored and very often rude.

Body language is very personal. It also conveys messages about one's character and respect for others. The meeting attendees may be feeling ill which could be the reason for inattentiveness. Have all the facts and draw an informed conclusion. Don't make assumptions one on one, in a group or from a distance.

We must remember to analyze objectively and avoid incorporating any personal bias which may cloud our influence, opinions or vision. Remember not to assume but that facts bring clarity.

# The Job Market Jungle

It's a jungle out there! Recruiters and job hunters alike are constantly on the prowl, in search of the perfect candidate or potential step-up career move. Some job hunters are desperate and every move they make is intended to attract decision makers.

What occurs after they have identified their target will certainly determine if they will bag the "big one."

If you are on the career hunt, the most important thing to do before you head out is to be prepared. Map out the territory. When you step out into the job market don't forget your "keys." Know where you are headed and take stock of your equipment. You have talent, technical skills, personality, principles and a strong work ethic. Hopefully, you are well mannered and know the "rules of the game."

You know you have these qualifications so go out and sell yourself. No one can do that for you. Think of yourself as a prepared hunter, meet people face to face and be ready to succeed.

Your résumé may get you in the door for your first interview but what happens after that is all about your preparation. A good hunter would never go into the jungle with out checking his map and gear, his hunting clothes and having his equipment in good working order. If you are an employed hunter, you must realize that there are a minimum of five other hunters stalking around waiting to take your job. Their backpacks are bulging with referral letters, recommendations, expertise and internships. Even if you are a business owner, there are at least five people who want to do what you are doing. They are honing their skills and practicing, checking their equipment and adding new equipment to their gear so they will be ready when the opportunity they seek is at hand.

You must distinguish yourself from the other hunters by doing what you do better than anyone else. It is no longer enough to hunt all day and work hard dawn until dusk. The competition is fierce and you need to outperform them in everyway.

Arriving for an interview in flip-flops, shorts or with your hair in rollers will certainly make an impression. The game is over before it even gets started. You are obviously hunting in left field. Your tattoos may be considered camouflage to you but in the jungle work place it's best to cover them up along with any body piercing ornaments used by the natives.

Learn to speak the language of the work force. You must be able to pronounce the name of the company you have targeted and also the name of the interviewer. Don't be loud or obnoxious. Your jokes may not be appreciated. You may frighten the "big one" away. And, don't talk too much. Be concise, clear and succinct respecting the time you have been given.

Be prepared to ask questions and let the interviewer know how you can be a value to the company. As a hunter, you have experience and leadership qualities which you need to use your unique personality to sell. You have skills and are interesting while all the time circumventing any discussion regarding how terrible your last job or management team was. Good hunters never complain nor do they talk about money or benefits during the first interview.

One cannot be too cautious when attempting to navigate the business jungle. With a sharpened set of technical skills and the ability to communicate with the Human Resources species while being "dressed to impress" or so the saying goes, should put your qualifications ahead of your competition.

Set your specific goals and focus on your mission. While in the jungle, keep your eyes and ears open for hazards, traps, and quick-sand. Be prepared and be ready to perform when called upon. You should do just fine, especially if you know the "rules of the game" and carry respect, along with you at all times, for the work environment and those you meet in the largest of all jungles ... the business jungle.

# Reputation

I must remind you that to succeed in the playing and winning of any game without practice, your chances of out performing your competition are diminished greatly. You must practice, practice and practice on every playing field available. The more you tend to the rules, (not bend the rules), and practice, the quicker you will become comfortable in any setting. Your image will be that of a person of influence – a professional.

The Greek poet Evenas left us these words, "Habit, my friend, is practice long pursued, that at last becomes man himself."

The rules of professional behavior need to be cultivated and polished. The more they are used, the brighter the gleam which attracts admiration from all those with whom you come in contact.

Your reputation is not built on things you are going to do. Reputation is built on things you do. What people *do not* do also creates a reputation. Some say "I know what to do, I just don't do it." What does that statement say about you? Loud and clear, the message is sent that you care more about yourself than your customer, client, friend, or spouse.

It is not about you, my friend, it is all about how you are perceived by others and it is time for you to "do it"!

When you respect those with whom you do business and spend enough time with them to develop shared experiences, you are in a position of trust. When your words and actions match, people know they can trust you.

Tom Peters writes, in his look, *In Search of Excellence,* "Always remember the person you are trying to persuade is at the epicenter of his or her universe. Treat him or her accordingly and you will have solved many of life's thornier problems." In other words, "Do it!" Practice! Never cut people short.

If you don't treat them with civility, they will eventually find a way to retaliate. You have no doubt heard the saying: "People are like elevators. They take you up, and they take you down."

Avoid the pronoun, "I." Instead, use "we." You very seldom do things single-handedly in business. You don't want to be branded as ego centric even if you have that inclination.

Also, never be condescending. Current customs assure every living person and creature a purpose, dignity, and a right to be respected. Being rude, loud, domineering, or arrogant at anytime, anywhere is totally unacceptable.

Show your own vulnerability. You're human after all and humble. You do make mistakes – granted it is seldom, but even you have not reached perfection as yet. When you are wrong, admit it. Being wrong doesn't mean you are less. If you fight to be right with your co-workers, you have given up a very strong suit – humility. "Please" and "thank you" are to be used often in business. "I'm sorry" also doesn't hurt when you say it.

# Where Have All
the Customers Gone?

Where have all your customers gone? Are new customers rare and hard to find? Could it possibly be your customer base is dwindling because of the way they are treated? You bet.

It is interesting to me when I ask the attendees at my seminars one simple question, they stare at me blankly. They ponder the question but the room is silent. The question I always ask is "Please give me the names of ten businesses with which you personally enjoy doing business. These are not businesses connected to your business, but outside your business environment."

It is a sad commentary, but never can an attendee name ten. I then ask for three and rarely can any one attendee give me three names but it does happen. Occasionally, I'll ask for one and I often receive several responses.

My next question is "Why do you enjoy doing business with this company?" The answers returned are never because of the product or service offered by the business.

The answers are almost always because of the way the attendee is treated. Never is it because the cleaners clean the clothes the best or the grocery has the best oranges – the bank has the best money – the auto repair shop changes the tires the best.

Usually the responses are "because they always smile when they greet me as though they are really glad to see me." Other common responses are "because they always go out of their way to help me," "they call me by name" and "they really appreciate my business."

It is a fact that customers like to do business where they are known, appreciated and respected.

Nordstrom's retail stores are historically known for legendry customer service. Being from Chicago, I kept hearing people rave about a store in California that gave fabulous customer service. This was 30 years ago. I boarded a plane and flew to California just to check out the customer service at Nordstrom's, a store born in the Northwest that I had never heard of before. To my delight, the rumors were true. I learned first-hand that reputation travels across country – good or bad. When Nordstrom's sales began to slip a few years ago, they called the Chairman of the Board out of retirement to get them back on track. It worked.

The Ritz-Carlton and Marriott have excellent training programs for their employees and Bloomingdale's customer service attitude shows marked improvement.

Manners do matter in whatever business or playing field you come in contact – especially *your* business.

What is the cost of loyalty? Businesses close daily and corporations spend millions of dollars training their employees, especially sales people, on how to be attentive to their customers.

Appreciation of a customer costs nothing and the residuals are priceless. A smile along with "please" and "thank you" really are not painful. It is an issue of common courtesy.

Break the mold; break the expectation of poor service. Give your customer your personal attention and give the hum-drum day of your customer, client or patient a boost. Become that energetic, delightful up-beat professional who really appreciates her business.

That customer can spend her quarters anywhere and your success depends on her wanting to give her business to you because you really care and appreciate her.

Follow up and follow through. A telephone call occasionally, to see if your product or service is serving your customer well, works wonders. A personal call to a customer you haven't seen for a while to let her know she has been missed is another way to make your customers feel their connection to you and your business. Of course, a hand written thank you note really is the ultimate in customer attention and relations.

Be honest with yourself. You know very well you have experienced customer "no service." Ask yourself to think of a business or two you enjoy and why. Now apply the same service attitude to your own business. Go forth and be fruitful. Your customer base will grow and loyalty will be your reward because you have given just what every customer really wants – your appreciation and respect.

# LEADERSHIP

# *Authority*

How easy it is for us to forget that authority is not a substitute for leadership. When one reaches the executive level of management, a certain amount of authority goes with it. Authority makes us feel important but if we use authority in a way that makes others feel unimportant it becomes poor management.

Sometimes it's really incredible what a little bit of power does to some people. When opportunity knocks and they move up a notch in status, they begin to act so full of themselves and superior you lose touch. They just give the orders and that's that.

When management dictates or gives orders, sometimes it is justified because a situation may require instant reaction the fastest way possible. But if it happens frequently, the ability to build a lasting feeling of cooperation and loyalty in people, on whom they depend, is lost.

Real authority cannot just be handed to a manager. To be effective, it must be earned. It is not the authority of a position or title that gets employees to perform well; it is their regard for the manager's competence, ability and the appreciation shown them. Being knowledgeable and highly competent will automatically create a certain measure of authority and trust. If those you lead look upon you as an expert on a given subject or field, they will normally let you exercise all the authority needed to get the job done.

Conversely, people who don't respect the competence or judgment of their leaders will follow their lead grudgingly, no matter how much they are pressured. They are likely to drag their feet, resist what needs to be done, become resentful, protest or even throw a monkey wrench into the gears.

A knowledgeable, highly competent executive will very rarely need to "pull rank," intimidate or call attention to their status.

Those who are confident that they can perform well find no necessity to impress everyone that they are "the brass." They always get better results and receive more cooperation from their associates when respect is given. These managers are well liked because they rely on reason and persuasion rather than by ordering people to do things. They command respect rather than demand it.

Some executives let their authority rather than leadership show as they handle disappointments. Voices are raised, tempers became short and their strengths and weakness are revealed. When things don't go according to plan, it can put to the test how steady and dependable an executive really is.

Despite our best efforts and intentions, we are all bound to be disappointed now and again but we can't offend or become unduly discouraged. Time is wasted trying to find someone or something to blame. Any executive worth the title helps people land on their feet when they stumble rather than make life rougher by jumping all over them.

Good leaders will, of course, always strive for perfection; however they cannot allow themselves to become absolute perfectionists. When employees make mistakes they should be corrected and even the best of managers occasionally overdo it. Some tend to notice the slightest imperfections or consider the day a total loss unless they can discover something that someone did wrong. Others are just plain stingy with compliments. They operate under the assumption that people need constant correcting. They take good work for granted and look for one or two things that may have been done wrong or differently.

Nothing discourages people more than to do their best and have their manager pick it to pieces. Drawing attention to employees' mistakes, no matter how trivial, may seem like a good way to keep them on their toes, but isn't nearly as effective as being certain to notice and appreciate the things they have done right.

Executives or managers, who are super-critical, set impossible standards, leave people discouraged, fearful and their confidence shaken. There may even be times when people have worked their hearts out, when it's best not to discuss imperfect results.

Leadership requires common sense to steer clear of failure but we must accept occasional disappointment as the price for progress. The executive hasn't been born who is clever enough to succeed at everything all the time, but the responsibility of leadership is to arouse an eager desire for the employee to follow the leader.

# U.S. Leadership

I f you take a look at this year's Fortune 500 companies, at the top of the list you'll find Wal-Mart Stores, a retailer employing 1.9 million people worldwide. Among the top 10 are petroleum, technology, automotive, banking and insurance companies. Of the 20 most profitable, you'll find UAL, the parent company of United Airlines that emerged from bankruptcy in 2006.

What do these companies have in common? They have incredibly talented and tenacious leadership who are astute, aware and yes, aggravating. Their role is to inspire and challenge everyone in their organization to constantly become more efficient, productive, innovative and customer-centric. They know what it takes to thrive and survive in the highly competitive global marketplace.

In reading excerpts from Lee Iacocca's new book, *Where Have All the Leaders Gone?*, it dawned on me that the people who "know," the leaders, are exactly where they need to be in business. However, consider how fortunate we all would be if they were serving our country in another way. Not in the military but someplace even more important – in the White House, in Congress and in every facet of government.

Have you ever considered that the United States Government is like a conglomerate? It operates a variety of businesses, has employees, a board of directors and shareholders, debt, profits and lots of competition.

The Government uses trade dollars, tax collections and other revenue sources to make loans and to pay thousands of vendors and trading partners. It also uses those dollars to compensate more than 2.5 million employees ranging from mail clerks and administrators to military personnel and executive staff whose combined annual payroll approaches a staggering $14 billion dollars. That's 14 with a B.

Our Government provides billions of dollars in goods and services, some $13.3 trillion globally, but also has a sizable debt in the trillions. It is publicly held by you and me... some 200 million voting-eligible stakeholders. I say voting-eligible because only 60 percent of us ever bother to vote.

The CEO is the President, who has a board of directors, the Cabinet. The members are employed to advise him on any subject relating to the duties of their respective offices.

It is generally agreed the most important single function of the Government is to secure our rights and freedoms as citizens, deriving its powers from us. While the original mission was clear, over the decades it has become unfocused, unwieldy and expensive. If a corporate CEO did this, he or she would be drummed out, especially if the solvency of the company were jeopardized. The stakeholders also would call for the board (Cabinet) to resign.

We all too often vote for or against a person because of their politics, personality or record of public service, not on their ability to truly lead. Nothing can substitute for experienced leadership. We should expect no less from those responsible for our government or its agencies.

In business, when a firm is not functioning properly, the leaders are empowered – no, they are obligated – to divest, reinvest, realign, reorganize ... to make the tough decisions that will ensure the future solvency of the company, the livelihoods of its employees and the profitability of its investors.

These leaders have decades of practice and proven track records of turning around poorly performing operations, launching new enterprises and winning the confidence of those around them. They are chosen, not for their charisma or connections, but for their ability, fortitude and vision; the keys which open doors.

One of America's corporate icons, Lee Iacocca, minces no words about our current state of government. While he takes serious aim at incumbents, I looked more objectively at his fervor for this county.

In relating his "Nine Cs of Leadership," Iacocca says they are the obvious qualities every true leader should have:

- "A leader has to show CURIOSITY." He has to listen to people outside of the 'Yes, sir' circle.

- "A leader has to be CREATIVE, go out on a limb, and be willing to try something different. You know, *think outside the box*." Leadership is all about managing change—whether you're leading a company or leading a country.
- "A leader has to COMMUNICATE." I'm talking about facing reality and telling the truth.
- "A leader has to be a person of CHARACTER." Know the difference between right and wrong and doing the right thing.
- "A leader must have COURAGE." Swagger isn't courage. Courage is a commitment to taking a position even when you know it will cost you votes.
- "To be a leader you've got to have CONVICTION—a fire in your belly." You've got to really want to get something done.
- "A leader should have CHARISMA." The quality that makes people want to follow you. It's the ability to *inspire*. People follow a leader because they *trust* him.
- "A leader has to be COMPETENT." You've got to know what you're doing and you've got to surround yourself with people who know what *they're* doing.
- "You can't be a leader if you don't have COMMON SENSE."

Finally, Mr. Iacocca suggests "the biggest C is CRISIS." "Leaders are made, not born. Leadership is forged in times of crisis," notes Iacocca. He questions who better to lead us out of trouble than someone who's done it before?

Thousands of ready made leaders are out there with the very qualities and qualifications we need. They know the protocols. The protocols of business are the "rules." Etiquette is being knowledgeable about the rules and what to do in any given situation and doing it with confidence. It's melding rules and skills to ensure a positive outcome. Leaders are masters of management etiquette. They know precisely what it takes to move an organization in a positive direction.

Every day, we hear of successful leaders retiring, writing books, going on the speaking circuit, becoming consultants or moving into philanthropic pursuits. Why not consider national service, corporate citizenship redefined and tackled with the same passion and commitment demonstrated as a corporate executive?

Our forefathers, the founders of our country, had fire in their bellies. Most were landowners, merchants, businessmen, who volunteered their time, with passion, as patriots, to write our Constitution and form a more perfect Union. They didn't do it for fame or fortune. They already had that just as the business leaders of today have.

Governors Mitt Romney of Massachusetts and Arnold Schwarzenegger of California each hold their offices without salary. They donate their time because they feel grateful for the opportunities this country has offered them. It is their form of giving back. The message to corporate and industry heads is that we need great leaders to step forward and give their time, experience and know-how to their country.

It is the ultimate in voluntarism by bringing their fire and commitment to Washington. SCORE, Service Corps of Retired Executives, to the tenth power! Let's move patriotism beyond the boardroom. It's time to pay the piper and pledge liberty, justice … and leadership … for all.

# Trust Management

As our career takes shape we are always eager to increase our leadership skills and level of responsibility. We read books, take courses and even bone up on the latest findings about human relations. These are great exercises as long as we don't forget one very important fact. No techniques, no matter how clever, can conceal the motives we carry in our hearts.

What do we really value in our executives? The majority of us want them to be honest, truthful, straight-forward and those we can really trust.

It is a pleasure to work for someone in whom we can trust with confidence. Likewise, it is always a problem if we feel we cannot trust our leaders.

Executives who long for a reputation of being trustworthy have to earn it. The first step is to show the same consideration for everyone – the weak, the powerful, loud or quiet, personal friends or those who are not favorites.

Be obvious, simple and straight-forward and say what you mean and mean what you say. People don't like double-talk.

One's reputation is built on action. Conversely, what management does not do also creates a reputation.

Sincerity and integrity cannot be faked, at least not for long. If leaders have the best interests of their employees at heart, it will show by their actions time and again and will build a reservoir of good will.

One cannot create a feeling of mutual trust with people overnight. It takes time and effort. Sincerity can't be turned on and off like a water faucet. Leaders who are sincere don't have to advertise the fact. Sincerity is visible in everything they do and soon becomes common knowledge to everyone.

Likewise, insincerity or skirting the rules cannot be hidden, disguised or covered up no matter how competent a manager may be.

The only way to develop good will and high esteem of those with whom you work is to deserve it. Each of us is eventually recognized for exactly who and what we are, not an image we are trying to portray but isn't real.

Good managers take a little more than their share of the blame when things don't happen as planned and a little less of the credit when all goes well. Always give those who work for you the credit that is rightfully theirs. To do otherwise is both morally and ethically dishonest.

The morale of a company team is more important than the size or amount of experience it has. When morale sags, so does performance. People can become disenchanted with their job for a number of reasons. A good salary is important but when they know that upper management is generally interested in them and their ambitions, good attitudes come naturally. They want to be appreciated and feel what they do is significant.

When a leader is aware of what the members of his team want, shows them that he or she cares, treats them with respect and appreciation on a daily basis, the team spirit is uplifted. With an honest and sincere attitude, by their leaders, employees will trust management and good morale will surely follow. Their needs have been met by a successful supervisor who has been sincere in praise and honest in its delivery.

# Follow-Through

I have often talked about business as a game. It is an exciting game filled with competition at every level, strategy, quick actions and re-actions, wins, losses and, of course, rules. The game of business is played locally, nationally and internationally with many of the same components as many other games.

The focus here is on follow-through. A good follow-through is just as important in business as it is in bowling, tennis, golf or baseball. Follow-through is the bridge between good planning and good results.

Effective managers must learn the art of delegating. When a savvy executive gives someone a job, the next step is to get out of the way and let them do it. The fact remains, however, that after the responsibility for the task has been given, it cannot be just delegated and forgotten. Some kind of follow-through is essential to achieve the best results.

Some very capable managers or leaders have a difficult time with this concept. They think very well, plan well and are good at delegating but then relax and are disappointed when things don't work out as well as they had planned.

When their visions have not been fulfilled, they question, what happened? Why did you do this or why didn't you do that? Blame is usually thrust upon the delegate when actually the blame for failure rests with the delegator.

Being creative and doing the planning or being the visionary are the fun parts of the game. Following up and methodically checking on the player's progress is an essential step for the effective executive.

Good managers will leave people alone and not stand directly over them as they do the job but they don't go away altogether and just keep their fingers crossed that all will go well. They stay in touch, help where needed, keep control and follow the progress. They always know the score because they are diligently keeping score.

Excellent plans don't assure excellent results. When the progress of a task is followed, there is less likelihood of a foul-up or foul out. The best managers get off the bench. They make certain the players understand what to do, the signals are straight and each player receives praise for a job well done!

# Hope and Faith

"Most folks are about as happy as they make up their minds to be." These words said by Abraham Lincoln hold me in good stead when things seem to be going in the wrong direction. I gather myself together, smile and put faith into action as I step forward, make some adjustments and take the road necessary to alter my course.

If we don't panic or let stress take over as the market falls and we find our jobs are in jeopardy, our savings shrinking and our future not exactly as we have hoped, we will fare far better than if we did not remain calm. As Americans, we know the best way to minimize our own problems is to help others solve theirs.

This may sound like pie in the sky to some, and it is true that things may get worse before they get better. Yet keep in mind that the majority of us have known and weathered hardships before and we can and will do it again. During the worst depression, men and women may have lost everything they owned except their character. They also kept faith when they thought all was lost and continually hoped their efforts would bring better times.

We are united and we know how to take the bitter with the better. There is no use ducking the issue or pulling the covers over our heads. Whatever you may be sure of, be sure of this: We are dreadfully like others in the very same situation.

Egotism and greed are responsible for some powerful and imaginative rationalizations. Each of us eventually is recognized for exactly what we are – not what we try to appear to be.

Greed and ego cannot be hidden, disguised or covered up no matter how high a position a company executive holds. One must deserve high esteem if it is to be awarded. In the long run, no techniques, no matter how clever, can conceal the motives by which people are driven. The right motives are much more important than the right moves.

To give real service and hold a position of trust, a leader must hold the interests of those they lead in their heart. Trust cannot be taught or measured with money except in the minds of the corrupt. Sincerity and integrity are qualities built into a leader and shown in his other actions time and again.

Some leaders betray themselves due to the selection of their associates. One must not forget that you are known by the company you keep. Unfortunately, some executives aren't all that concerned about the welfare of their people, but want only to use and manipulate them. No matter how glib or charismatic such people are, or how clever as amateur psychologists, their motives are bound to show through eventually. Oh, they smile the smile and talk the talk, but we usually become suspicious when sincerity doesn't "feel" genuine. The glass ceiling now has a major crack in it and, as seen recently, it has come tumbling down.

Now we must pick up the pieces. We have learned to check references and acquaintances carefully. We must question, challenge our leaders and company executives while checking past records to see that they have made real contributions and not been merely job-hoppers. Human resource officers have found that the credentials posted in a resume are often fictitious. Some high-level executives take liberty with the truth just to make their credentials look better. They are invariably caught and released from their positions. It is a shame, but since it has become more prevalent we must be more diligent. Our faith has been bruised but not destroyed.

As the ones we thought were our leaders fail and disappoint us, we must continue to have hope because hope looks for good in people; it discovers what can be done instead of grumbling about those who have disappointed us or what was or cannot be done. Hope pushes ahead when it would be easier to quit and it lights the candle to see the future instead of cursing the darkness and what was. Hope stimulates our attitude and puts those smiles on our faces that affect all those around us as we go forth, become fruitful again and create our future success.

# Personal Ambition

I heard a story about a Chicago physician who did research on ulcers and had to abandon the use of dogs in his experiments. The reason was not that PETA caused him to stop but the dogs themselves. They simply were not ambitious enough. They refused to get tense and worry which, at the time, was thought to be the cause of ulcers.

If you inflict an ulcer upon a dog artificially, he will sit down and very placidly cure himself by refusing to be bothered about anything.

In thinking about this story, I came to realize the lesson. Our lives are more complicated than a dog's and our needs are greater. We must be ambitious to survive.

Executives or managers who aren't ambitious aren't worth their salt and shouldn't really be leaders in the first place. Those who are overly ambitious or ambitious in the wrong way hurt their own chances of success and they may just ruin their health at the same time.

When we let personal ambition dominate us, we lose our perspective. If our ambition is greater than our ability we also become victims of constant tension and frustration.

We strive to get ahead and competition is a driving force in the game of business. Those who lose even a part of their inner drive run the risk of sitting on the bench.

Human desire to succeed or win is one thing but preoccupation with personal ambition is another. It tends to keep us constantly wound up and frustrated, and carried to an extreme it becomes a stumbling block to our progress and our own peace of mind.

We learn the hard way that being ambitious, not for ourselves but for the organization, is most effective. We are rewarded or paid by the organization to be ambitious. The more successful we are, the more obviously valuable our services will be.

Being ambitious for the company is one of the best ways for leaders to show their talents and receive greater rewards and advancement. Resorting to politics or internal feuding is not professional etiquette and is never an option for getting ahead, that bigger office, more authority or being paid more. Here are some common symptoms of over-ambition and over-competitiveness:

> Trying to build up the importance of our own job and lessening the importance of those of others.
>
> Refusing to extend wholehearted co-operation that others need to do their jobs well.
>
> Sniping, backbiting and criticizing.
>
> Fostering obvious personal rivalries between people who can't seem to agree on anything.

Envying the success of others will not get us anything except perhaps a painful hole in the lining of our stomachs. We must adopt, adapt and stay emotionally well-balanced while concentrating on doing the very best job we possibly can.

It is a mark of intelligence, no matter what you are doing, to have a good time doing it. Remember the dog and that all animals, except man, know the principal business of life is to enjoy it. Don't let personal ambition become a pain.

# Barking Dogs

"A fast moving train does not stop for barking dogs" is a statement I have made more times than I can count. I believe it and use it even when I'm alone and motivating myself. Yes, I talk to myself on occasion.

When you set your sights on your ultimate goal and focus totally on your destination, you should let nothing slow you down, stop you or derail you from reaching your objective.

As I watched the 2010 Winter Olympics, I couldn't help but think about each Olympian and the drive and focus each had to make it to his/her destination.

The hours of practice, the sacrifice, the pain, disappointments, doubts and difficulties disguised as barking dogs did not diminish their desire or stop them from reaching Vancouver. Their train was always on track and moving forward.

Your train or personal goal, when up to speed, is fueled by powerful motivation. Even though there are circumstances and disappointments or barking dogs along the way, if you are truly focused and determined, you will not stop until your destination is reached.

Ask yourself if your motivation is passionate or a mere whim. How serious are you about your career or are you just doing your job?

Don't forget that in today's global competitive business arena, putting in an eight hour day, being technically trained or earning an MBA is not enough to get you where you want to go.

These are tools you do need but ultimately your own desire, motivation and love of what you have chosen as the direction of your career will drive your focus and acceleration.

Others will want to ride on your train with you if they trust your direction and in your ultimate destination. How you are perceived by these "others" will ultimately determine your success or lack thereof. No matter how streamlined your train may be, it cannot operate by itself. If those "others" don't want to come aboard, your train will be stuck in the station or stopped time and again.

You must pay attention and realize the speed and direction of your personal train is propelled by your focus. I know that you will never meet a rich, mentally competent hermit. You must depend on yourself, but you need the help of others to enable you to reach your destination.

The Olympians reached their destination, and be assured there were many "others" on board – coaches, sponsors, medical advisors and cheerleaders. Parents who drove them to and from practices, who paid for lessons. Some made great personal sacrifices to ensure each Olympian's personal train got to where it should go.

Invite others to get on board your train, and when they do, make certain you put yourself in high gear and don't let anything stop you. The barking dogs of negativity, jealously and criticism will inevitably be in your path. Stay focused on your destination. You know where you want to go; stay focused and totally motivated, and never allow your train to stop for barking dogs.

# SAY WHAT YOU MEAN AND MEAN WHAT YOU SAY

# *Watch What You Say*

In business there are some words and phrases, we don't want to hear and are better left unsaid. I'm not referring to "You're fired" or "We're downsizing." Of course, word pollution or the use of foul language is at the top of the list. Using profanity in the workplace is disrespectful under any circumstances. It displays the lack of communication skills so necessary for the successful businessperson. It also shows the listener that you have a temper problem and are undisciplined.

Very few of us take into much consideration our choice of words we tend to use daily. Nor do we analyze the effect especially negative words have on those with whom we are communicating. We just talk.

It always brings a smile to my face when I hear someone say, "Thank you for having me," as they offer a thanks for an invitation. The host or hostess didn't have YOU. They had mashed potatoes, roast beef and green beans. Only cannibals have "you." How about "Thank you for the invitation" or "It was a pleasure being with you"?

Do you realize the word "No," for example, should never be uttered in the business arena? You never thought of that did you? We tend to use it constantly even though none of us particularly enjoys hearing it.

I find it somewhat amazing that most people will accept anything negative you have to say if you begin with a positive and end with a positive. I didn't say they would like it but rather that they would accept it. For example, instead of saying "I don't know" one might offer, "I'd like to know that myself. I'll find out."

Another way of saying "No" but in the positive is with a statement. For example, question, "Have you ever been to China?" Instead of saying "No," I suggest, "China? I've been to Canada, Mexico and Europe. China is next on my list of places to visit." You have said "No" without actually uttering the word.

Certainly it takes thought to change what you say negatively into pleasant positive responses. We must exercise our brains and when we do, everyone benefits. If you will listen to yourself and become aware of the many negatives you use during the day, you'll be surprised.

Here is that word "Hi" again that sounds anything but professional. Imagine a little child, just beginning to talk, looking up at you and saying "Hi." Do you really want to sound cute and infantile in a business meeting? Opt for "Good morning," "Good afternoon" or "It's nice to see you again." Yes, it does take some practice.

When you say it, you sound it. Better to check your vocabulary. Use words like good value, higher quality, or wise investment rather than "It was really cheap." Use your vocabulary properly to enhance your meaning. And beware that using large words might be heard as condescending. Choose your words wisely.

Business is non-gender and ageless. Most everything is based on status and position. Terms such as "boy, girl, honey, sweetie or sweetheart" are insulting, derogatory and certainly out of place.

In the business arena, there are several topics to be avoided which are known as hot-buttons. Gossip, the cost of personal items and notoriously heated issues, which should be reserved for private company such as: religious beliefs, abortion, immigration, the legalization of certain drugs, and the war in Iraq. In a bi-partisan office environment, politics or political slurs about a candidate or one currently holding office should be off-limits. Avoid conflict – don't arbitrate it.

Lapel buttons, armbands, sashes, anti-AIDS emblems, save the whales and breast cancer ribbons, no matter how valid the cause are not appropriate business accessories.

We all have problems, including your co-workers and management.

We also have many wonderful things happen in our lives, on occasion. It is very difficult to restrain ourselves to keep either of these situations to ourselves; however, it should be business policy.

Sharing your private problems at work makes you appear laden with misfortune. It is not the strong competent professional image you want to project.

Conversely, if your children make the Honor Roll consistently or your social life is exciting and full, you also need to keep this information private. You may be very fortunate and others within the company are very likely to see you as boastful. The green-eyed monster of jealousy and envy might rise up from the depths to hit you where it hurts – in your career.

Just keep in mind that it is better to watch what you say, how you say it and when and where you say it. I leave you with this thought. Some conversations, often meant to be private, travel through the air vents in the washroom, and may be overheard. Hmmmm!

# Foul Language

In every city and village, the outcry is the same: "Where did it go? We want it back." Desire for etiquette consciousness is infiltrating the core values of our people. There is an awakening to the thoughtfulness, consideration and respect that reflect the words and actions of our heritage.

Unlike the previous generation, today we actually pay to attend movies where our families, friends and most of all our children are pummeled with words and story lines that socially do not raise our standards, but reverse the trend for excellence in all that we do.

Like it or not, management equates good manners with competence and bad manners with incompetence. A vital component to business success is not only being familiar with the rules or protocols of the game, but also playing by those rules. The rules are merely a part of the game, but without them, playing the game properly and winning are out of the question.

Knowing the rules of the game of business are not enough. For example, if you were to go out onto the basketball court and begin reciting all the rules of the game of basketball, players around you would be making baskets, gaining points, and you would lose. On the other hand, if you were playing the game and not playing by the rules, you would foul, foul and foul again, eventually fouling out altogether and ultimately losing.

You may be just as technically trained as your competition, but to become a leader, you must have self-confidence. To win in the game of business, you also need communication and presentation skills, consideration and a healthy dose of respect for yourself and for those with whom you come in contact. You need to do whatever it is you do even better than your competition. You must "outclass" your competition and create the desire for customers and clients to want to do business with you because they are welcomed, known, appreciated and most of all respected. Anything less is just plain foul.

# The Rules of Engagement

W hen you first hear the expression "the rules of engagement" what comes to your mind? Some people may possibly think it has a romantic connotation connected with a marriage proposal. Others might relate the expression to terms of engaging the enemy in wartime. This chapter is not heading in either of those directions. If we stretch really hard, we might be able to find a thread of connection.

The engagement we are addressing today is art of engaging in conversation. How you can become thought of as a bright conversationalist who is charming, witty and a joy to invite to any function.

Even if you don't have a sparkling personality or a quick repartee handy at all times, you can develop a comfortable style all your own just by following these few guidelines:

1. Watch your body language. Don't fold your arms across your chest or stand with your hands crossed in front of you, in the fig leaf position. If you do, it shows you are defensive. Never put your hands behind your back, in the "at-ease" stance. The message you are sending is that you are lacking in confidence. If you put your hands in your pockets, it conveys a casual uncaring attitude. Don't lean on anything – not a chair, a table, wall, window sill or desk. You immediately lose your power.

When seated, don't turn your back to the person sitting right next to you. Even if you are listening to the person sitting on your other side, it totally excludes the one looking at your back. Make certain you are inclusive rather than exclusive.

2. When you shake hands, look directly into the persons eyes and say the name. People love to hear their own name. It also helps you remember the name while giving your full attention. If you have the opportunity,

use their name during the course of conversation. Even a simple, "Good morning, John," rather than "Good morning" does wonders for your image. You personalize your greeting. Of course, "Good morning" is better than saying nothing at all.

3. Ms. Barbara Walters, one of the most famous interviewers of all time, says to "just ask questions and get the other person to talk about themselves." You will be the one thought of as interesting. Ask open-ended questions beginning with why, what, and how rather than questions which can be answered "yes" or "no."

4. Don't forget your breath mints. They are as important as your wallet and your business cards. Just having them with you is not enough however, you must use them frequently. Gum is not an acceptable substitute.

5. Be current and well-informed. Read the *Business Journal* and daily, in your area regularly and also keep up with weather, sports and international issues. Small talk is necessary at any function. If your mind melts, try Eleanor Roosevelt's method. It is said, she had to converse with so many dignitaries, being the wife of the President, she would use the alphabet as a brain tickler. She would begin with the letter "A" and say something like "Apples are so perfect this time of the year. What is your favorite apple?" If the other person responded, "I don't like apples," and offered nothing more, Mrs. Roosevelt would then go to the B's or C's, right on through the alphabet, to engage in conversation.

Some subjects to avoid are your health, the cost of things, mean gossip, off-color jokes and controversial issues particularly if you don't know where others in the group stand.

6. Never be condescending. Current customs assure every living person and creature a purpose, dignity and a right to be respected. Being rude or arrogant at anytime, anywhere is totally unacceptable. Don't forget anger begets anger. Self-control and diplomacy are professional necessities. A positive upbeat attitude will also garner you the recognition you desire.

7. Be a good listener. Part of a good conversation is listening. Don't disengage prematurely. Good listeners are engaging and generally very popular people.

8. Don't speak in a foreign language in front of or over other people who do not understand, unless your words are being interpreted. Along those same lines, never whisper in front of anyone. If you must talk privately, leave the room.

9. At a dinner event, try to sit across from your spouse. You will then be talking with two people, on your right and your left, and your spouse

will also talk with two people. You both are much more interesting. You will avoid the inclination to only talk to your spouse during the meal. The saying "turn the tables on you means to make certain you talk to the person on your left during the first course, then, turn the tables so to speak, and talk to the person on your right during the second course.

10. Eliminate any regional accent, if possible, and develop charisma and energy in an unpretentious way. Most radio and television personalities have a mid-western way of speaking, free of regional identification. Be soft-spoken yet confident. Women should practice lowering their voices which have a tendency to rise in pitch, especially if they are excited or nervous.

11. Be generous with praise, especially in the company of others. Don't flatter anyone to the point of being phony or insincere. Remember, a gem is valuable only when it is genuine.

12. Finally, use the statement "oh, there you are!" It makes another feel important. I also suggest you begin a sentence with, "I really enjoy …." It makes a great lead-in and people want to listen. Don't forget to smile freely. Smiling is contagious; spread yours around and start an epidemic.

Doing business in the competitive marketplace today requires excellent soft skills. By being engaging you leave your professional mark on yet another touch point.

# Self-Expression

Recently I saw an advertisement with the main point reading "What Matters Most is How You See Yourself." If you have read my nationally syndicated column or my other books, you know I totally disagree with that premise. Are you a tiger or a pussycat? It doesn't matter how you see yourself. Most of the time you don't see yourself as others see you. And, there in lies success or failure.

It is not about you and how you see yourself – it is all about how others see you and their perception. Some leaders in industry begin to fail because their focus turns inward on themselves. They once had a total laser-like focus on what they needed to do and they were visionaries and thought big. After they reach their goal, they become doers rather then leaders. Some become comfortable and are distracted by the trappings of wealth, notoriety and even celebrity.

When we speak of professionalism, we must always consider what is being communicated. Leaders must avoid believing that the staff can sense their goals even without being told. Misunderstanding usually comes from negligent communication. Don't become full of yourself and don't assume everyone knows what you mean. Be clear about your message and leave no doubt. When achieving results becomes more important than how the results are achieved, there is trouble brewing.

Do you realize that past successes create tremendous pressure for management? John Tillitson, an archbishop of Canterbury in the late 1600s, wrote, "They who are in the highest places and have the most power, have the least freedom, because they are the most observed."

If fear of failure drives management, often mistakes of others are magnified. It is difficult, at times, to look inward and ask yourself if, in fact, your communication was lacking. It is easier to immediately jump to the conclusion that errors were made by others, when actually, it was your own communication negligence to begin with that really caused the problem. Sometimes stress or fatigue is the culprit that causes us to lose our temper and say things which negatively impact our position as a leader. We unfortunately treat others with a lack of respect. We also receive what we give. Kindness begets kindness and respect begets respect.

I have bitten my tongue more times than I can count. I have also just reacted to a situation and looked inward after the fact, and wished that I had done that first. I believe that's called Monday morning quarterbacking. I have learned that if frustration becomes an anger problem, I must hold on, "bite my tongue," and look inward before I speak.

It is imperative for management to constantly subject itself to scrutiny. What you believe about yourself and how you behave may often be in conflict. Manipulation and leadership can slip back and forth crossing a fine line eventually effecting and possibly eroding ones integrity and good judgment.

If you let your integrity lapse your self-control, good judgment and leadership skills have been compromised. In other words, never cut people short or lash out in anger. Of course, your blood pressure will rise and you will be angry from time to time, but be aware, that your own failure is knocking on the door. If you are in a management position, manage yourself!

Check your communication skills regularly to avoid disaster. Your business environment should be enjoyable and fulfilling. Bring your sense of humor with you and communicate with clarity. Love what you do and respect your followers. You will find they will do all the more. Become a cheerleader instead of a drill sergeant. Smiles and compliments make everyone feel good and you will be perceived as the leader you think you are.

# Listen for Success

Y ou have begun to read this page for at least two very important reasons. Number one, and most important, your interest in improving your business acumen. Second, your belief in my expertise based on the previous keys we've shared and my credentials.

It all comes down to adult curiosity in a subject of interest to each of us. Let's keep it simple. We both want you to reach your career goals quickly, smoothly and faster than your competition.

Of course, this combination of facts causes me to immediately like you. You are willing to read this important key and listen and digest to the written word as I share my experience with you. Good listeners are extremely popular people. Everyone likes a good listener.

We meet many people throughout our lifetime. Some are very pleasant acquaintances with whom we have much in common – bowling league, school, church, gardening, golf, etc. We then select a few acquaintances, a very few, with whom we have great rapport, to actually become our treasured close and trusted friends.

Just think for a moment about your dearest or best friend. What attributes do you share to qualify you as "best friends"? You no doubt have common interests, consideration for each other, respect, trust and you listen to each other.

John D. Rockefeller is quoted as saying, "I will pay more for the ability to deal with people than for any other ability under the sun." If you develop your "people skills," you will not have the same lament as John Rockefeller who was lacking in his ability to listen and therefore he was not popular, or even well liked, by those he most wanted to impress.

Technical skills and knowledge account for 15 percent of the reason you get a job, keep a job, or advance in a job. Eighty-five percent of your job success is connected to your people skills. These percentage figures are based on research conducted by Harvard University, The Carnegie Foundation and the Stanford Research Institute. We are judged time and time again, like it or not.

The eyes have it! The mood, tone and direction of a business encounter are set in the first three to five seconds. Make those initial seconds count to form a positive impression.

Your eyes can project confidence, sincerity, trust, approval, enthusiasm, joy and excitement. They can carry negative emotions as well. Don't make people feel put on the spot or uncomfortable. Don't allow your eyes to focus on part of a person's body other than the face. Make good eye contact. It shows you have a sincere interest and are not merely going through the motions while trying to appear polite.

Try to be well informed. You might read at least one daily newspaper along with a weekly news magazine. Before attending an event, be prepared to discuss items of current interest: books, films, television shows, sports, political events – anything that is in the news. Bring up one of these topics during the first lull in conversation and then sit back and listen. Others will be grateful to you for filling in the silence. Ask open-ended questions that require explanations, not a "yes" or "no" reply. People enjoy talking about themselves – so don't hesitate to ask them. Avoid asking boring questions such as, "Do you enjoy working at the bank?" Instead, ask them what they like about working in a bank. Some subjects that you should avoid when you don't know where others in the group stand: your health, the cost of things, mean gossip, off-color jokes and controversial issues.

Another quote which is apropos by Epictetus – even before my time – is true forever more: "Nature gave us one tongue and two ears so we could hear twice as much as we speak." Listening is twice as hard as talking. Let whomever you're talking with finish his conversation or make his point.

Don't interrupt or talk over someone. I call it "quietus interruptus." You hear it all the time on television and radio talk shows. So many people are trying to get their opinion expressed all at the same time; you can't understand what any of them are saying.

This reminds me of the "talking feather." In meetings, Native American men were given a feather and permission to speak by the chief. A brave would talk without interruption as long as he held the "talking feather."

When he was finished, he would pass the feather to the next brave, who would then talk without interruption

In a meeting, if you need to make a point and another person insists on talking without relinquishing the floor, stand up. The chair is obligated to recognize someone who stands and your action will signal the other person that he or she has talked too long.

Think before you speak. Form your ideas and include pauses and silences. You will then appear to be thoughtful. Look directly at the person with whom you are speaking and give them your attention. Women have a tendency to nod in agreement as they are listening. Men do not, which sometimes gives the impression they are not listening when, in fact, they really are.

Finally, always close a conversation. Don't walk away from a person without bringing the conversation to an end.

We've touched on respect, consideration, thoughtfulness and your clear objective should be confidence in yourself at all times. If you practice using these keys and incorporate them into your daily business regimen, your popularity will soar and your career goals will become a reality much sooner than you ever expected. Listen! I do believe I hear success knocking.

# Political and
# Religious Discussions

L et's talk about political views and religious beliefs in the office. Are you kidding me?

As passionate as you may be about your political views, the discussion of politics is out of place in a non-partisan business environment. A business meeting should never be used as a bully-pulpit to voice political opinions. One must be very cautious and avoid even "slipping in "a comment about a sitting government official or one on the campaign trail.

Political lapel buttons or those advocating one cause or another are off-limits at the office. Sashes, armbands, anti-AIDS emblems, save the whales, and breast cancer ribbons, no matter how valid the cause, are also not appropriate business accessories.

Etiquette seeks to avoid conflict, not arbitrate it. Understand that employees and associates must practice their political and religious beliefs privately, without intruding on others within the workplace. They must be allowed the freedom to worship God as they understand Him. I agree with actor, author and television commentator Ben Stein's view that nowhere in our Constitution does it say America is an explicitly atheist country. That having been said, religion and one's politics are personal choices and should be reserved for conversation or debate outside of the business arena.

As a considerate meeting chair, don't schedule a meeting on Friday afternoon or on the eve of a major or religious holiday. The optimal words here are considerate and sensitive.

Whether in the workplace, the break room or the company washroom, consideration and respect for others' viewpoints must be adhered to. It makes no difference, or shouldn't, if one is liberal, conservative, Democrat, Republican, Libertarian, Atheist, Agnostic, Muslim, Protestant, Catholic, Buddhist or Hindu, just open the company mail and get on with the business at hand.

By all means, share the Girl Scout cookies but be very leery of asking for donations for your personal charitable causes.

If your company, as a unit, opts for an outreach to the community by supporting a charitable endeavor with volunteer hours of service or a matching fund donation, the choice is yours to participate or not. Keep in mind the outreach program should not be religious or political in nature.

An employee should never feel intimidated, demeaned or threatened with the loss of a job, if politics are discussed and opinions are not in step with their supervisor's.

When attending a business lunch or dinner outside of the company environment, avoid the subject of politics, especially if you do not know the political leanings of those present. Even though the coming elections may appear to be timely, the subject or perhaps even an off-the-cuff, snide remark about a sitting official may not be well-taken.

Avoid off-color jokes or ethnic references and don't spend time knocking the competition. Discussing strategy and how to gain an upper hand in the competitive market, out-smarting or out-classing the competition certainly are appropriate subjects but demagoguery, name-calling or derogatory comments about the competition or anyone are unnecessary.

Keep abreast of current events such as international issues, weather and sports. General conversation or small talk takes place during the beginning of the meal and the solid business discussion begins with the dessert course. Then the papers come out and down-to-earth business is discussed.

Remember to keep your cell phone turned to silent and off of the table, along with your eye glasses, car keys, purse or anything else you might even think about placing on the table.

Often when dining over a business meal, we fall into the comfortable environment of the social get-together. Beware! Because you are out of the office and having a business meal, you may become too casual and your "best" becomes less than apparent.

Competitive business takes place on many practice fields and in arenas all over the world. I read recently that it doesn't matter what you talk about when offering "small talk." I beg to differ. It does matter, a great deal in business. For example, if you ask personal questions, such as "Where do you live?" or "Are you married?" your dining partners may be quite offended. They may ask, "Why do you want to know?" In business, personal questions are none of your business.

Don't become a casualty of global competition. Embrace diversity and be sensitive to the freedoms we all enjoy. At the same time, keep religious, political and personal choices just that – personal and private.

# INTER-OFFICE
# COMPATIBILITY

# Corrective Criticism

Just recently I read that eighteen people committed suicide in three months, and they all worked for the same company. It seems that the negative atmosphere in and around the company was so intense, the employees became depressed and felt totally hopeless.

In this decade with job loss at a high point added to the loss of savings and retirement benefits, it's no wonder many in the workforce are fearful and edgy.

Management must reach out to employees to make certain the work environment is cohesive and confident. The team needs a good locker room pep talk and uplifting evaluations of their performance.

Despite management's good intentions, often excellent managers let their own insecurity reveal itself in how they choose to express themselves.

The manager who criticizes is seldom forgiven, but one who encourages is seldom forgotten. Words of praise are all well and good, but an employee will take home and take to heart negative comments. It generally takes two positive statements to erase one negative one. Negative comments stay with us for a long time, whether or not we deserve them. Unfortunately, they also stick together to form a lack of confidence and foundation of self-doubt and a feeling of futility.

George Bernard Shaw's quote, "A critic is to art what a pigeon is to a statue," seems to say it perfectly.

Respect is key and if you have to offer a negative assessment, be careful not to be on the attack. Because a habit needs to be changed or a distracting problem corrected, does not give license to select degrading remarks.

Constructive criticism should be a spring board to growth and improvement. Being polite and supportive will have a positive impact on the employee's attitude and willingness to achieve the desired outcome.

It does no good if an employee feels degraded or embarrassed and wants to quit. Everyone loses: the employee is out of a job and feels terrible about himself, the employer lost a well-trained employee, the customer doesn't get the benefit of service from an employee with a great attitude and the company has lost a good customer and a good employee because a manger let personality override respect.

Keep the environment for corrective criticism lighter, brighter, relaxed and purposeful. Depression is not conclusive to good business, but respectful expression of suggested improvements is. Attitude is everything!!

# *Apology – Magic*

Have you ever been seated in a restaurant a half hour or forty-five minutes later than your reservation? Is an "I'm so sorry" offered? How about giving the apology some substance with a complimentary glass of wine for your inconvenience? Why is it so difficult for people to say "I'm sorry" and really mean it? I have observed that many don't know how to apologize or what to say. Often it doesn't even occur to an offender that an apology is even necessary.

Many people resist offering an apology because it entails admitting fault. Often the effect is just the opposite because it diminishes the anger of an aggrieved party, and fault is not questionable. An apology is like magic, but resistance to it persists. In her book, *The Argument Culture: Moving from Debate to Dialogue*, Deborah Tanner points out that in public discourse human relationships are modeled on a metaphorical battle between two polarized sides like a shoot-out between two gunslingers – one must lose and the other side wins.

Where is the magic in that? Yes, we seem to be in an argumentative culture where the fear of losing becomes permanent. Apologizing can seem all the more like a defeat.

Insurance companies advise us to "never admit fault" if you are involved in a fender bender. You may want to say "I'm sorry," but substituting legal procedures for a simple apology can create even more frustration. The magic of an apology works in many ways. Surprisingly, the offended party may be prompted to admit fault. Apologies are the equivalent of a handshake and often come in pairs. I'm sorry for X, and then you are sorry for Y and consider the matter closed.

Don't value aggression over conciliation. We have many ways of saving face and getting along in our society. That's how communication works. It also explains the power of the seemingly simple but deeply satisfying act of an apology. Using the magic of two simple words, "I'm sorry" one can save a less than perfect interaction.

As children we learned the two little magic words (actually three), please and thank you. As adults, let's add two more magic words that should be used often: "I'm sorry."

# Attitude is "Everything"

How well you distinguish between working, socializing and schmoozing will directly affect your career.

Some days are going to be better than others. Going into the office and meeting "Chatty Cathy" just inside the door can be daunting on those days when your head is pounding. You know her, the one who is always happy and smiling while talking incessantly in that high-pitched voice that grates on your nerves. She is the same "Chatty Cathy" who on other days brings a smile to your face because hers is contagious.

How you handle stressful conditions can have a great bearing on your opportunities to be promoted. Do you add to the tensions of interoffice incompatibility, or are you good at diffusing them? You can change the office climate by making simple, positive words and gestures a part of your vocabulary.

When you arrive, set the tone with a cheery "Good morning" and smile, even though your heart is breaking, or so the song goes. A positive impression almost always follows a warm greeting.

Most people can accept anything negative you have to say to them if you begin with a positive, end with a positive and drop the negative in the middle. I didn't say they would like it, I said they can accept it. Have you stopped to listen to all the negativity you spread and receive from those with whom you associate on a regular basis? The words "No," "I don't know," "I can't," "I won't" and "Not now" are just a few examples of what you say and hear regularly. Bummer! How about changing the "No" responses to "Yes" or the "I don't know" answers to "I'll find out," or each "I can't" to "I will"?

Don't forget "please" and "thank you." Be courteous and complimentary. Acknowledge contributions with "Great job" or "You've helped me a lot" or "That's a great idea," or be a team player with "May I help you with that?"

Your positive attitude will help others lighten up their attitude – and believe me, attitude is *everything*! You can give an employee more training to increase skill, or more education to increase performance, but attitude must come from inside the individual. People are totally in charge of their choices regarding their own attitude. No employer can afford to retain an employee with a bad attitude.

How many of you reading this today have ever worked with someone or for someone with a bad attitude? I'll bet most of you answered that you have. A bad attitude is like a rotten apple in a barrel. It will ruin all the other apples. I have a plaque in my office that reads, "If it's going to be, it's up to me." That saying very clearly addresses itself to one's attitude.

Good behavior doesn't come with entitlements. When things don't go your way, keep your self-confidence and temperament intact. Avoid exhibiting hurt feelings or holding a grudge. Being grumpy just because you feel like it doesn't work well either.

Mean gossip and personal innuendo should also be avoided at all times. Some employees actually start false rumors about a co-worker just to put a glimmer of doubt in the minds of management about that person's character, morals or abilities. Sarcasm, criticism, blame and the belittling of co-workers or management personalities or style will generally ensure you a trip ticket – a pink one.

Perfection never helped me reach my goal. If I do my best and try to master new skills, carry a positive, goal-focused attitude, and strive for harmony in my life, I must give in to the idea that I'm going to make mistakes and have days that go down in my journal as something less than desirable. I've always learned from my mistakes, and it's amazing just how many wonderful ideas come from others.

The image you convey and the etiquette you practice will be major determinants in how well you achieve your personal and professional goals. In other words, these are your skeleton keys. Be certain you build and keep good relationships and prepare yourself. And one day, you will be the boss.

# Packaging Yourself Professionally

# The I's Have It

"I don't want to wear a tie." "I know how to dress." "I don't think manners matter." "I'm a very casual, laid-back kind of a guy." "I don't want to be stiff and formal." "I live in a warm climate."

Have you heard these comments? We all have, time and time again. Notice it is always the same. These statements begin with the overused pronoun "I."

It's not about you and the fact that you are a laid-back kind of a guy who likes to dress casually. Your right to do just that is not being challenged or revoked. It is, however, about how you are perceived by others – the "others" being those who hold the keys to your successful future.

If you want to appear to be a rube among the Rolex set, that's fine. Perhaps you don't realize that your blatant disregard for your "professional" appearance will cost you dearly in the long run.

You don't have to be stiff and formal. Formality is not the comfortable professional look that is particularly desirable.

The contemporary attitude in corporate America today is still technically oriented. Social skills used effectively, prior to the manners deficit so evident today, are high on the priority list of those in upper management. A candidate applying for a position is encouraged to do most of the talking during the interview to enable management to discern the level of proficiency in the candidate's communication skills. Excellent interpersonal skills enable employees to work in a diversified environment.

You see so much rage today – road rage, air rage and just plain old rage. On a daily basis, we experience discrimination, industrial-strength rudeness and the blatant lack of even the simplest acts of courtesy.

It is time for each of us to stop and reflect on the things we know, but are too caught up in the "I" or "today" syndrome to bring out of the training we had in our past and put to use. Examples are pride in our appearance, courtesy, thoughtfulness, respect, civility, honesty and yes, ethics.

In this highly competitive arena of business today, your talent and technical skills are superb qualities to have but, like it or not, management equates good manners with competence and bad manners with incompetence even during the interview process for entry-level positions. Manners *do* matter.

In the words of motivational speaker and author Jim Rohn: "There is probably no sphere of human activity in which our values and our lifestyles are reflected more openly than in the way we dress. The power to inspire, control and even manipulate those with whom we come in contact lies in the decisions you make regarding how you choose to package yourself."

How do you choose to package yourself? Are you thoughtful about your appearance and do you select your wardrobe to reflect your business presence? Are you packaged to call attention to your many assets, to do your best and at least try to do it better than anyone else? Are ethics, honesty and character a part of your package? What do you see when you look in the mirror? Are you dressed for business or for golf? Do you see a confident, well-prepared, considerate representative of your company?

Remember, we seldom see ourselves as others see us. Look again. And before you go out the door, check your attitude … and reach for your keys.

# *Business Cards*

In business circles, networking events are popular and most often very well attended. Recently, I attended a very successful event hosted for women only. Although the bevy of women was friendly, enjoyed themselves and was there to promote their respective businesses, for the most part they missed the mark on business card presentation. Business cards were passed around like flyers at a hardware store opening. The need to address this issue leaped at me again, as I observed the lack of business card protocol offered by these well-intentioned women. They just "didn't know."

The following guidelines were motivated by these women, but men must realize business is non-gender and business card protocols apply to them as well. You can do irreparable damage to your business and your professional image merely by incorrectly presenting your business card to the wrong person, in the wrong way, at the wrong time.

Some guests weren't in business but had high hopes for the future. If one is not in business, a calling card would do the trick in place of a business card. A name and phone number on a simple white card is a boon to single women who either are not in business or don't want to scribble their name and phone number on a cocktail napkin. This type of card is also useful to drop in the clear fish bowl for the inevitable give-away drawing.

A calling card is used in some instances as a business card. For example, in the military, the person's name, rank and military branch are listed on a plain card. A calling card with just your name is also used socially in formal situations, in place of a business card. The card may be given to a protocol officer prior to entering a receiving line for introductory purposes at a diplomatic dinner. It may also be placed on a silver plate near the front door in a private residence, to say that you had stopped by, in a rather old-fashioned custom mostly seen in Europe. Of course, you," as one who knows," would never just "stop by or drop in," without calling first to make certain you are welcome and to learn what time would be convenient.

Your business card is part of your visual communications package. A handsome business card properly presented makes a lasting impression. Please don't confuse your business card with one which has your picture on it and a list of things you do, awards you have earned along with clever sayings and multi-colors. That would be a mini-brochure.

Your business card should reflect your good taste. Very often management will supply you with company business cards printed for you and you have little to say regarding the way they are designed. If you do have a choice, your card should be printed on good quality card stock, in white or ecru, with black or dark blue ink. It may have a small company logo in the top corner but preferably not splashed across the card. In business everything is based on status and position, never age or gender. Keep your card simple and it will signal your professional acumen. As your status increases, your business cards should be engraved and classic.

Never present a card that is soiled, crumpled, dog-eared or out of date. If your e-mail or any information on the card has changed, have new ones printed immediately. Don't present a card with numbers or information crossed out. Tell the person, you don't have a card with you but you will be happy to send him one at the address on his or her card. Then send your newly printed crisp card…the one which reflects your professional image.

Remember, a junior in status should never give or request a business card from a senior in status. If the senior in status or position wants your card, he or she will ask for it. If you want your card in the senior executive's hands, handwrite a note saying it was a pleasure meeting him at the XYZ event. Enclose your business card. Now it is in the hands of the executive, along with a personalized handwritten note and an offer to be of service. This makes a positive and memorable impression.

Be selective about those to whom you give your card. Giving your card to anyone and everyone makes you appear pushy and unprofessional. However, always carry a good supply of business cards with you and keep them within easy access. It is wise to carry business cards in the evening at social events as well. An occasion might arise when you'll be glad you carried your cards.

When traveling to another country, have your cards printed in the language of the target country and printed in English on the other side. Also, have a good supply printed not just a few because it lets those in the country you are visiting know you are serious about doing business with them.

Speaking of other countries, we learned a lot from the Japanese. For example, we learned to ask whether you may present your card. The Japanese also present their card with two hands, one on the top of each corner and with a slight bow to show respect. We don't go quite that far but we have learned to present our card with the print facing the recipient. When we receive a card, now we take the time to actually look at it when it is given. It is a thoughtful gesture but also helps you remember the person's name and the name of the company.

Never write anything on the back of the card in front of the giver. After you walk away, privately you may jot a pertinent note on the back of the card, if you must. If you have colors and printing on the back of your card it leaves no space for writing anything. Tossing a card on a desk or saying, "here's my card," and the good ol' boy slap on the back way of doing business is no longer acceptable in today's global community. "Here's my card" was heard repeatedly at the networking event I talked about earlier. Whether or not I wanted the card was of no matter. I got one anyway. I was never asked if I wanted the card. It goes without saying most of the unsolicited cards ended up in the circular file.

Never produce a card at a private luncheon or dinner where you run the risk of your host seeing the exchange and do not force your card on anyone or offer it early in a conversation.

In an office, as a visitor, always present your card to the receptionist when you arrive. This makes a good impression, helps him or her remember you and your name. Don't forget the receptionist is also the gatekeeper.

In a business meeting, where several persons are present, either here or abroad, place the business cards you receive on the table in front of you. It helps you keep the names, faces and positions straight. Often pre-printed tent cards will be placed in advance for seating and recognition purposes by a thoughtful meeting chair.

No matter if you are in the United States or abroad, always present your business card before serious discussion begins ... never at the end of a meeting.

Finally, invest in a good carrying case to hold your business cards and keep them clean and crisp. Don't put your cards in your pocket without a case because bringing them out of your pocket to present, along with lint or candy wrappers, is definitely not considered good form. And, now you know what others don't.

# Your Paper Package Wardrobe

How you package yourself is important when it comes to your attitude and personal wardrobe. You have another way of packaging yourself which is equally visible and important to your success.

Your paper package! You send or give the paper package of yourself in your business cards, your stationery and everything you send through the mail or share with those you meet.

You know you shouldn't present an outdated, soiled or dog-eared business card to anyone. We are now going above and beyond the initial gesture to a much greater professional opportunity.

The graphic image of your company to the outside world, if you work for a large company, is dictated by their logo, design, paper quality and color choice.

You, on the other hand, are totally responsible for your own image and good taste. What you send under your own name to colleagues, friends and contacts speaks volumes about who you are and your personal professional presence.

Small business owners must realize that well-designed stationery and paper packaging plays a major role in the business image you want to create and in ones personal success.

It is important, even for the employees locked in to what is made available by their company, to take responsibility for their own personnel stationery and its quality.

You always want to co-ordinate all your stationery. The coversheet for letters and additional blank pages should match in color and quality. The envelope should also match and be large enough to hold a check.

Always put your telephone, fax number and e-mail address on your letterhead in large enough print to read. It certainly makes it easier for someone to contact you.

If the glue on the envelope is old or insufficient, don't use scotch tape to seal the letter. Invest in a glue stick.

Fold the letter or invoice in thirds and place it in the envelope with the top fold down. When the recipient removes and opens it, your business information and graphics will be seen first.

For the conservative business you certainly don't want to appear cute or faddish. White or ecru good quality paper is best. Remember, as in all things, when in doubt opt for formality.

For a contemporary look, once again, good quality paper is the best choice. Smoky or light colors may be used for certain businesses such as design firms, ad agencies, restaurants, automotive etc.

Lettering should be dark blue or black for the conservative business and a deeper contrasting color that works well with the paper choice for the less formal business image.

Whatever design you choose to convey your business identity, be certain to carry it through from your business cards to stationery to company signage and even 5" x 7" note pads used in the office.

As you ascend the corporate ladder to the Boardroom, you may well consider engraved stationary. It is the ultimate in quality, a visual statement of luxury and is a pleasure to receive. Usually in large companies you don't have options. Your business cards and stationery are supplied either printed or engraved depending upon your status. In most companies only senior management has engraved stationery.

If you are in business for yourself, don't hedge on quality for your business cards. Your handshake and business card remain as your professional self-expression. If you are thought of as unprofessional your business will definitely suffer. If you work for or own more than one business each business should be represented by a separate card.

Your card should include the following: Your name and title, company name, business and fax numbers P.O. Box and e-mail address. No pictures of yourself please. Besides being more than slightly egocentric, a picture on a business card is a security risk, especially for women. What are you selling or who are you representing? Don't diminish the business. Instead make yourself memorable by your professionalism. Your business card should not be a substitute for an advertising or promotional brochure or look like one.

Correspondence cards are a must-have in your paper package. They are used for personal correspondence, thank you notes, invitations, congratulatory messages and expressions of condolence. Your choice of correspondence cards acts as a reflection of your personal good taste. Having them doesn't count. You must use them regularly. Generally, they are a fold-over, 4 ½ x 6 inch card in ecru or white stock of high quality.

Considered classic, the notes may be engraved with initials on the front, embossed or foil-stamped with either name or initials. My personal notes are done by a heat process called thermography, which causes the ink to rise slightly for an engraved feel without an engraved price tag.

When an executive attends a meeting, luncheon, dinner or event to which he/she has been invited, a thank you note is handwritten and mailed immediately. Some savvy executives write the note even before attending the event and drop it in the mail on the way back to the office or home. The word handwritten is key here. A typed or e-mail thank you is not appropriate. The note must be handwritten. An e-mail, as a second form of appreciation, is well-received but it does not take the place of a handwritten note.

Notes should never be printed with the words "thank you" on the front. You express your thanks on the inside of the note, not with a commercial "thank you" on the outside for any invitation or gift.

Invest in a good pen for signing your letters, notes and contracts. Taking out your trusty plastic ball point does nothing for your professional presence even though it does get the job done.

Package yourself in every way possible to reflect the image of your business and yourself as unified and professional.

# Your Voice: An Asset or a Liability?

I s your voice relaxed and easy to listen to or do you have a pitch so sharp people wince? Is your speaking pace so fast even a professional auctioneer would have trouble keeping up? If you find that people don't understand you or are tuning you out perhaps your words are running into each other on the way out of your mouth.

Do you sound authentic and natural or is your speech pattern borrowed from another era, country or region?

Actors often try to sound urbane with Ivy League overtones, gentrified with augmented vowels and consonants. If you go overboard with enunciation or affection you may be seen or heard as arrogant. My best advice is to keep your voice real and congenial.

Listen to yourself after you have recorded a few lines of your favorite poem or book. You can do that with your voice mail message. Listen to yourself and adjust what you say so the caller can hear a smile in your voice. To create your personal message you do it over several times to get it to sound just right. You see, you do care how you sound; at least on your voice mail message. You need to go a step further and even tape a short conversation.

You may be surprised at how you really sound to others when you are not creating the perfect voice mail message.

A man's deep voice may sound very attractive especially if he is a good communicator. However, the same voice may sound angry if not tempered. Some men will answer a phone abruptly and tend to sound like a drill sergeant.

A woman's voice if high-pitched can sound caustic or weak. Some automobile TV commercials are perfect examples of a woman's high-pitched. Public speakers have the same female challenge. When a woman is nervous or excited, her voice has a tendency to rise higher and higher until some actually begin to sound like Minnie Mouse.

As a public speaking coach, I work with many women on their presentation skills. I was training one woman in particular who took my advice to the extreme. She practiced lowering her voice and speaking clearly that she unfortunately sounded breathy and as though she was seducing everyone in the mostly male law office in which she worked.

It does take listening to your voice and some practice to reach the desired affect. Learning how to breathe properly can work wonders. Controlling your breath is especially helpful if you are nervous or have a weak voice. Adjusting your speaking pace will also help. Low voices sound muffled and a harsh loud voice may be over-whelming or threatening. Practice until you've learned to strike a balance.

Do you choose your words to inform or impress? Using a $20 word when a $2 word will do proves one thing-you are pretentious. Do you inflict obfuscation into an otherwise lucid statement for the sheer joy of watching someone squirm when they clearly don't understand what you said? Are acronyms DOA or are they an alive and well part of your vocabulary? Unreeling sentences saturated with shortcuts will clog up any channel of comprehension. A reader can revert to a point of reference to refresh what an acronym means; a listener can't. While attempting to recall the meaning, the next sentence or two may slip by completely unheard.

How do you ask questions? Are your questions direct or convoluted by transitions multiple part and tangents? Does one need a road map to figure out what you want to know? And, how do you answer questions? Are your responses to the point and succinct or do you ramble on to ad nauseam.

If you are a business owner, how you express yourself will set the tone for your company. Not only is your message important but also the style and clarity with which you offer it.

If you are a supervisor or manager you may have excellent aptitude, but your ability to earn respect may center on your attitude and the allegiance of employees or how you choose and use your words to guide, mentor and motivate them.

Words can be pitiful or powerful. The choice is yours. Your voice and how you use it can be as asset or a liability. Whether you are talking in person, on the phone, on a teleconference, or in a room full of colleagues, always be clear, concise and considerate. Then be quiet and see what feedback you get. Communication is excellent when it is used in two directions – the giving and receiving of information. Being a good listener is equally important.

# Director of First Impressions

The key here is the focus on two very important support persons: the receptionist and the executive professional assistant.

The person who generally has first contact with the customer or client is the receptionist. He or she represents the professional image a company wants to project and spends a great deal of money to achieve. The advertising budget of many companies is totally useless if the customer immediately gets the wrong impression.

Just think of the power the receptionist wields. Usually, this person answers the phone, fields questions and complaints, greets clients and directs traffic, while totally representing the company every time the phone rings or someone comes through the door of the business.

A well-trained professional receptionist has excellent communication skills, dresses well, has a pleasant personality, is customer service oriented and knows the company business inside and out. She is without question an invaluable asset and the company is indeed fortunate if she is also bilingual.

Am I dreaming? Definitely not. These qualifications may seem to over-qualify some job seekers; however, they are really quite realistic.

I pray not to offend and I do realize that men also handle reception duties. The same rules and qualifications apply to either gender; however, since the majority of receptionists are women, I am using the feminine gender in reference.

Unfortunately, often managers fail to realize the receptionist should be one of the most knowledgeable persons in the company. I didn't say the smartest or the most technically proficient. I said knowledgeable.

Some companies hire a cute little "space cadet" and give her 10 minutes of training in the use of the phone system, after which they give her a list of names and extensions and consider the training complete. So often the position is considered strictly entry-level and even the employee thinks of herself as "just a receptionist."

A professional receptionist should be trained in every department of the business and be able to answer most of the questions posed by a caller, before ever taking her place as the primary person who answers the phone. This valuable employee, when trained properly, knows how each department operates, who does what, when they do it, how they do it and who does it when the primary contact is not available.

The receptionist is also the gatekeeper. As a visitor, always present your business card to the receptionist and mention your appointment time as well as the name of the person you came to see. Make a good impression on the receptionist and be respectful. When she is answering a call, be patient and don't talk to her while she is talking on the phone. She can't listen to two people at the same time. Try to smile and make a pleasant remark. If two people arrive at the same time, the pleasant one that made her smile will get by the gate first. Guaranteed!

The professional executive assistant is another gatekeeper. She is the executive's right hand. She keeps the boss on schedule and knows where he is and when he will return or she should know.

One of the main complaints of the executive assistant is that Mr. or Ms. Boss leaves and doesn't say when he/she will return, which leaves the assistant uninformed. That is a definite no-no. The second highest on the complaint list about the boss is that he/she doesn't return phone calls. The clients are left to believe she has not given the boss their messages. Voicemail has helped but, the fact remains, phone calls should be returned.

A savvy assistant will have the same qualifications as the receptionist but with a few more five-star capabilities. Clients like to do business where relationships are established. The professional executive assistant knows how to contribute to the establishment and cultivation of those relationships. For example: An excellent assistant might keep a file, on 3" x 5" cards, with trivial information about the client such as "has a 7-year-old in Little League" or "sailed the America's Cup Race." When the client comes in for a meeting, the assistant impresses the client by asking about the son's Little League season or if he plans to race again. The personal touch adds to the feeling of value. Don't forget people like to do business where they are known, valued and respected.

The executive assistant knows when meetings are pressure-filled and seems always to be able to save the day with the last-minute details, reports, copies or aspirin. This professional keeps the schedules, meets the schedules and often creates the schedules, makes reservations, has reservations and represents the company well and her boss certainly.

Once a working relationship between the executive and the assistant has been established and expectations have repeatedly been met by both parties, trust is formed. Confidence in each other contributes to a well-oiled axle providing momentum and freedom for the executive to do what he or she does best – drive the company forward to the next goal.

The professional receptionist and executive assistant, for the most part, are undervalued with limited recognition for their importance to the success of the companies for which they work.

As I have woven the tapestry of my life, I have held each of these positions. I am very aware of the training necessary to be the best and not merely do the job. If you hold either of these positions and training has not been provided, then seek it. Don't sit back waiting to be spoon-fed information. Ask questions and experiment. Find the answers on your own. Take pride in what you do and become better than expected. It is not enough these days to put in a hard day's work. You must do your job better than anyone else, earn the raise, become invaluable and outclass your competition.

# Wardrobe Choices
## for the Professional

The successful business person, who wants to project an executive presence, must consider wardrobe choices. For business what one wears should reflect classic styles rather than trendy. Many of the current styles such as shirts which are not tucked in and sequined fabrics are out of place in a professional setting.

Women should take note. Wearing ultra-hip clothes and spike heels will garner you a great deal of attention and certainly get you noticed, however, you will also be remembered for your apparel rather than for your ideas or how well you do your job. The word "modesty" seems to be archaic in today's vocabulary. Cleavage exposed on a date is a matter of personal choice. In business, the choice is not an option. While magazines tout wearing a lingerie top under a jacket, it is a professional slip-up (no pun intended).

Tennis pro, the late Arthur Ashe, once said," Regardless of how you feel inside, always try to look like a winner. A sustained look of confidence can give you a mental edge that results in victory."

In business your stellar reputation will definitely add to your level of success. The visual impression you make will contribute to the conclusions people draw about you. Inappropriate attire will damage your reputation almost as fast as being poorly groomed or lax about your personal hygiene.

Both men and women should take a look at their shoes. Your shoes and their care make a statement about your attention to detail. Brown shoes with blue or black trousers or skirt shout "mistake." Check the heels on your shoes as well as the shine. Are your heels scuffed or run-over?

Men should trade in their sneakers and thick-soled wing tips for leather thin-soled shoes, not loafers. Leave your colored loafers and boots, even half boots, in your closet.

Women should wear closed-toed shoes with a mid-heel and hose. Bare legs, open toes (with toe rings or without) flip-flops, sneakers, spike heels and fishnet stockings are not appropriate in the business arena. Even if your flip-flops are Via Spiaga originals, they don't belong in the office. Brightly colored toes and feet, in need of a pedicure, are a fashion misstep. Make certain your panty hose are run free and have an extra pair handy as insurance.

Men need to get it right too. Out with the tie clips and school rings. Your fraternity pin should stay in the jewelry box along with your bargain watch. Select a good quality watch or two (one gold and one silver) not a sports watch. Bracelets, necklaces and pinkie rings are very 80's and a major turn-off.

Silk ties are a must in the executive wardrobe. Even though most ties are silk these days always opt for woven ties rather than printed ones. And please, throw out the novelty ties decorated with martinis, stick figures, the Mona Lisa and Santa Claus. Don't even wear them on "casual days." Ties set men apart and those who wear them are more likely to get attention.

A man's suit comes in three color choices which are best worn for business. They are navy, grey and black with different shades being acceptable. Stay away from earth tones and light colors, such as olives, browns and beige and also avoid plaids and checks. The suit is strictly for serious business, but for social business a brown sports coat works well and, on occasion, even jeans and a navy blazer are acceptable for the contemporary business man at a very casual event. The jacket means a man cares about how he looks.

Nothing looks more powerful or handsome than a white shirt with a navy or gray suit. To me, the white shirt also pairs well with a navy sport coat and says, 'I'm in charge.' By the way, the shirt cuff should show about a quarter of an inch below the sleeve of the jacket. If your jacket sleeves or trousers are too long, a little alteration will do wonders.

A men's tailor in whom I have great confidence tells me that men under 5'8" should consider trousers with no cuffs and they should never wear a three- or four-button jacket. I never knew that and I hope this bit of information helps. He told me about trousers with cuffs and no cuffs and where the break should be, but honestly it was more information than I needed to know. If you need more information, check with the tailor at a high-end men's clothier. They are usually up-to-date on pleats or no pleats and can answer most of your questions.

I know for certain that one should never wear white socks, unless a medical problem dictates otherwise, and avoid white shoes. The focus will be on your feet. Remember, your face is your communication center.

Don't buy jackets that are too skimpy. If a double-breasted jacket is your choice, don't let it hang open and flap. The double-breasted jacket is meant to be buttoned.

Finally, don't forget your shirt or jacket pocket is not your tool box. Don't stuff them with pens, rulers or pencils. It gives you and unkempt look and makes your jacket bulge over your stuffed shirt pocket. Your personal appearance makes a statement and is the key that opens doors. What is it you want to say about yourself when the door opens?

# Dress for the Occasion

What did you wear to your job interview?

When you are hired, the company buys your resume, your experience, your communication skills and your appearance. Yes, the company buys how you look, sound, and the value you will bring to the organization. It has made a sizeable investment in you.

You are now being paid to look or dress the way you did when you came in for your very first interview. Question? Why is it that within a few weeks after being hired, some employees take it upon themselves to change their appearance?

Instead of a tie and sports coat and slacks or suit with a coordinating tie, the employee changes the dress code to a golf shirt and khakis or jeans. Some wear sneakers instead of dress shoes. I've even seen flip flops and open toed sandals with brightly colored, ringed toes in professional business offices.

I was called in to an administrative office when desperation took over management. The CEO called me for help complaining that employees were ignoring the fact that the professional image of the business was in jeopardy.

Some employees were coming to work with pierced eyebrows, noses and one woman who answered the phone and responsible for, in many cases, the first contact with the company, had a pierced tongue. What in the world is that all about? None of the pierced appendages were visible when the initial interview took place. The company didn't buy that look as representing its professionalism.

I agree that sometimes what to wear can be confusing. Those in sales have a more difficult time because they often call on blue collar construction or maintenance personnel as well as executives. They don't want to appear overdressed or stiff to a construction crew while another group requires a more executive presence.

One must consider that the corporate culture or the type of business generally dictates appropriate attire. Use good judgment, but keep in mind that neatness counts, as well as personal hygiene. Raise the bar on your job performance as well as your appearance.

The following are some guidelines you will find useful:

**Business Attire**
<u>Women:</u> A blouse and skirt or golf shirt, big shirt and khakis or jeans are too casual. Women should wear closed-toed shoes with mid-heel and hose. Bare legs, open toes, flip-flops, sneakers, spike heels and fishnet stockings are not appropriate. The classic tailored look is professional.

<u>Men:</u> A suit or sports jacket and tie along with polished shoes and a good belt are definitely "in." Kinky or trendy attire is not considered fashionable in business except in the kinky, trendy, fashion business.

**Casual Attire**
Casual dress is to be worn only for barbecues, patio or pool parties, picnics, casual dinners and sporting events. Slacks are appropriate for men and women, but jeans should not be worn.

**Informal Attire**
Informal attire does not mean casual. The word "informal" means business attire before 6 o'clock in the evening. A dressy suit for women and a coat and tie for men are appropriate. After 6 o'clock, women may wear a dressy dress or a long or short cocktail dress, while men should wear a business suit with a tie.

**Formal Attire**
Formal attire dress means dressy dress or suit for women and a dark suit for men before 6 o'clock. After 6, the formal dress falls into two categories: black tie and white tie.

## Black tie Attire

Black tie attire means men should wear a single or double-breasted dinner jacket with a silk bow tie. A tuxedo or tux is the same thing. Military personnel wear an equivalent uniform. Women wear long or short evening dresses or evening separates.

## White Tie Attire

White tie attire is full evening dress. Men wear a long black tailcoat and white pique bow tie, and women wear their dressiest, most elaborate long gowns. The military wear the appropriate uniform.

## Gloves Attire

Gloves attire is worn more often in European and Latin American countries than in the United States. If you do wear gloves, remove them to eat or drink, and also remove the right-hand glove for shaking hands in a receiving line.

A.W. Combs said, "The maintenance and enhancement of the perceived self are the motives behind all behaviors."

It's not about you, your comfort level, your casual taste, or the fact that you want to wear your baseball hat backwards. It's all about how you are perceived by others in business. Man and women should opt for formality when in doubt. You can always become more casual. But if you arrive dressed too casually, the damage is done.

# Hats Off to You

In the years prior to the polyester leisure suit, businessmen very often wore hats. It was a common gesture of courtesy for a man to tip his hat when he greeted a woman, or remove it when he entered an elevator. The newsreels of earlier baseball games show men and women "dressed" to attend the event, hats and all.

Very few men wear fedoras or hats these days. Baseball caps and cowboy hats seem to be the head toppers of choice for men of all ages.

You may have noticed when the male professional golfers receive a hearty round of applause from the gallery, as they make their appearance on the first tee or make a great shot, they gesture a sign of appreciation. They tip or touch their hat or cap in recognition of the crowd and as a form of thanks for the applause and cheers from their fans. When one tips his hat or removes it, the message is sent in a mannerly fashion that respect is given and appreciation acknowledged.

Of course, I have heard and you probably have, too, that the name for the game of golf came about by using the acronym gentlemen only – ladies forbidden. I do not know who started that malicious falsehood which has traveled the globe for years. I do know, however, that the game was originally played by men and was/is known as a gentlemen's game. The game is played by the "rules" or the "etiquettes" of the game, which are strictly adhered to wherever the game is played. There are a few noticeable exceptions on some public courses, where men and women who don't know what is considered appropriate behavior are observed in various stages of undress.

Today, "what you don't know but others do" also seems to apply to the wearing and removing of a hat or baseball cap. Men really are out in left field on this one. The rules are much easier for women since we don't remove our hats or tip them in greetings.

We females have hats and caps in various styles, shapes and fabrics for any and all occasions. We wear elaborate hats for horse races and cowboy hats to the rodeo or even the beach. We wear baseball caps with almost any outfit, some with sequins, buttons and bows.

We wear hats to the grocery store, to sporting events, to our house of worship, while gardening, in the shower and sometimes even to bed.

Unlike men, we never have to remove our hats unless we want to. There are no protocols, that I am aware of, that dictate a woman must remove her hat.

Conversely, men wearing hats or caps must or at least should remove them when entering a place of worship (unless the religion dictates otherwise), an office, a political arena, a home, a restaurant or any private event held indoors.

In public places, such as the grocery store, shopping malls or sporting events, men may keep their hats on and should keep their shirts on as well. It is a matter of sanitation with the shirts. We'll discuss bare chests and bare feet at another time. Right now it's hats off to men!

Young boys who will someday yearn to be successful in their chosen careers should be taught, early on, to remove their hats in a restaurant or another's home. Grown men, of all ages and persuasions, are seen wearing baseball caps, some sideways, some backwards in restaurants thinking (or not thinking) it is all right because our society has become so casual today. Casual means without a jacket – it has nothing to do with your hat.

When our National Anthem is played at a ballgame, the players remove their caps and place them over their hearts. Football players remove their helmets. In sports, most men were taught, even in Little League, to remove their caps.

It isn't that we live in a more casual society today. Let's be honest. It is all about the fact that we are less respectful today. Being respectful by removing one's hat seems to be much less important than what is on the menu. Some restaurants and grocery stores even have felt the need to post signs reminding people that shirts and shoes are necessary for admittance.

We stand for the playing of the National Anthem, but look around. Men and women are seen talking and joking around. Some men leave their hats on because they just really don't care. That's not casual – it's disrespectful. Men, take a clue from the players. Remove your hat and have your son remove his.

Just because you are not "working" doesn't mean you leave your good manners and respect at the office or at home. Manners are not something you put on as you do your "Sunday best." Manners should be a part of your character. Dig them out of the closet, dust them off and begin wearing your good manners again. When you remove your hat, you will set an example for your children, be a symbol of pride to your own parents, and just maybe contribute to the raising of the level of civility among those with whom you come in contact.

It may seem like such a "little thing," but along with the hundreds of other "little things" respect needs to be given, received and appreciated. Manners are a matter of observed behavior. It's not about the fact that you really just don't want to remove your cap. It is all about civility and respect. Where did it go? We want it back! Hats off to you! We're watching and your character is showing.

# An Audience Member or Speaker

**Are you a courteous audience member?**

First things first. Please, turn off your cell phone when you enter the building or put it on silent. It's important to give a speaker or performer an opportunity to succeed without distractions. At a business meal, it is inappropriate to move about the room or ask for your coffee to be replenished after a speech has begun.

Keep your napkin in your lap while a luncheon or an after-dinner speaker is speaking. No one wants to look at your soiled napkin. Don't open candy wrappers or crinkle paper while listening to a speaker. If you must leave before the speaker or performer has finished, please slip out of the room as inconspicuously as possible.

It is certainly a joy to laugh at humor and the response is welcomed by the performer. Oh, I know we become enthusiastic and sometimes emotionally involved; however, it's not about how you feel. It is a matter of consideration for the speaker as well as the guests in the room.

Audience gestures and vocalizations can often be misconstrued as "coaching" or "heckling." Audible comments or mechanical sounds may be misinterpreted or distract the speaker. Additionally, make certain that no gestures are visible to the speaker, such as waving of arms, head movement or stomping of feet. While most speakers might enjoy your enthusiastic encouragement, courtesy demands that we listen intently and show our appreciation or disdain *after* the speaker has relinquished the platform.

### Are you a courteous speaker?

When giving a presentation or delivering a speech, you represent not only yourself but your organization. Just think how many millions or even billions of dollars companies spend on advertising and creating the very best image.

Speakers, do you consider the audience? Is your microphone adjusted properly? Do you wear appropriate attire? Do you think in advance about where the lapel microphone will be placed when you select your wardrobe? Women especially have a problem when it comes to microphone placement. Be certain to take into account that the lapel microphone comes in two pieces ... one for the lapel and one for the power source. Where do you place the power unit when you are wearing a one-piece dress? Will a lapel mike attach to a bare shoulder? With a standard microphone, make certain it is pointed at your chin.

Speakers should dress for success with jackets buttoned, shoes polished, hair groomed and apparel pressed. Shoes are important and should be appropriate for the occasion. If a jacket or sport coat is worn, it should be buttoned when the speaker approaches the platform, but may be opened during the speech.

To mention name badges briefly, speakers and hosts should remove their name badges before addressing the audience. Name badges often reflect light into the eyes of attendees. Name badges, especially those hanging around your neck, detract from your appearance and you certainly want the audience to see you and hear you at your best. We don't need to see your name badge. We already know who you are.

Your gestures should enhance your presentation. Never hold onto or lean on the lectern. It is not going anywhere. You give away your power when you use the lectern as a crutch. Never cross you hands in front of you in the fig leaf position. It shows you are defensive. Never put your hands behind your back. You are not representing the Armed Forces in the at-ease stance. It shows rather a lack of self-confidence. Never put your hands in your pockets. It shows a casual, uncaring attitude. Never use the "queen" gestures. Waving the left arm to the left and the right arm to the right makes it appear to the audience that you are shooing flies or perhaps revving up to take off. Do make your gestures count and visible to the audience, not close to your body so your audience can't see them. Don't just tell me – show me!

Being thoughtful and considerate as a speaker, performer or guest sets a positive example for others and reflects well on your organization and you.

# Your Name in the News

M ark Twain said, "Let someone else toot your horn and the sound will go twice as far." People like to hear their own name and also see their name in print. The company name along with theirs in a news release is even better. Publicity is one of those intangibles that is hard for some people to grasp. Used for centuries, the press release has evolved from the town crier. If it is done **correctly,** it can impact the bottom line every bit as much as a successful sales call. Who is going to know or want what you have to offer if they aren't aware you exist?

Unlike paid advertising, where the object is to extol the virtues of your product or service, the news story provides information about you or your business that allows consumers and decision makers the opportunity to make informed decisions in the marketplace.

Even the owners of the tiniest of businesses should seek out publicity because it is good business. It builds the reputation and credibility of the enterprise. No matter what your area of expertise there are several dozen competitors in the business arena groping and vying for the same customers as you. Huge companies have entire departments churning out informational releases with dizzying frequency. They know, and you should too, there is not a more cost effective way to reach the masses than through publicity.

You are perceived as an authority voice if you are quoted often. If you keep your company's name before the public you build name recognition and readers will remember who you are and your product or service easily.

Morale is enhanced in your workplace because employees feel a sense of pride when their names and photos are in print announcing job promotions or an award. Since you took the time to care about them, their productivity increases and so does profitability.

Getting your name in print however, can be as challenging as obtaining capital without collateral. I did say that getting publicity correctly can impact your bottom line so here is some timely advice.

First and foremost be considerate of a reporter's or editor's schedule. Don't call on a Friday and if you do call simply ask, "Are you on a deadline?" If the answer is yes, set an appointment to talk when it is more convenient for the editor or reporter. You will be appreciated and remembered.

While you may be eager to get your press release out of your computer and into the business section of some publication, your odds are much better if you do the preliminary work.

Make certain your press release is relevant, compelling and appropriate to the publication you want to run it. If your news is local, *USA Today* is not going to be excited about it. Make the news event actually newsworthy to people other than your mother.

Don't use big words, if small ones will do. Send your press release out on your company letterhead and never use fancy borders, or silly clipart. As for fonts, Times New Roman 12 point is easier to read than script. Include your contact name, phone number and e-mail address. A quote by somebody in your business adds credibility to the news you are addressing. Before you hit SEND ask yourself these questions:

- Is the release clear and easy to read?
- Is it interesting and accurate?
- Did I run spell-check and use proper punctuation and paragraph breaks?
- Is the final copy worth reading and would I read it if someone sent it to me?
- Why should the public care about your news?

After you send your press release, be accessible, cooperative and colorful in dealing with the media. Return phone calls and be sensitive to deadlines. Keep your attitude positive, your responses intelligent and enthusiastic. If you have anecdotes or analogies, be sure to share them so as not to sedate the journalist.

Finally, respect the reporter or editor. Keep the press releases to a minimum and be very selective about the ones you send. Don't be a pest by calling or e-mailing constantly. Keeping in touch is one thing but badgering is an etiquette no-no.

After all, your logo should not create a negative knee-jerk reaction; you don't want reporters using your press releases to make paper airplanes. If you call too often, send too many releases or are a nuisance, you may just get your real news overlooked.

As a professional yourself, it is to your advantage to build good relationships with reporters and editors, even if you have nothing to report.

# MEETINGS

# Board Meetings

Recently, an observation came very clearly into focus, for me, as I was invited to attend several meetings. There seems to be a ritual performed at most of the meetings. Not a conscious ritual but repeated actions that need to be given attention and examined for attitude adjustment and some fine-tuning.

I found it interesting watching some attendees come into various rooms with great anticipation, looking forward to an enjoyable learning experience. Some seem to gravitate to friends while others look for a comfortable chair, in just the right spot. There are those who enter the room, sit down, looking neither left nor right, silently almost stoically waiting for the meeting to begin.

The savvy meeting participant needs to personally address the following guidelines when attending or conducting a business meeting.

Each attendee should help create a friendly supportive atmosphere. Greet each other with the ultimate greeting – the handshake – and offer a genuine smile. The environment, which is set prior to the meeting, sets the tone and the responsibilities of the participants do not begin with the sound of the gavel at the opening of the meeting.

The savvy meeting Chair conducts the meeting, regardless of the level of seniority of the participants.

Meetings are a way of life in the business arena. Leadership requires that decisions are to be made thinking in the long term. What is decided in the meeting may greatly influence the future of the organization and those beyond its boundaries.

When you are the meeting Chair, begin with introductions. Welcome visitors and introduce those who don't know each other. Always stand for introductions whether introducing participants or being introduced. Be certain that you set a policy of inclusion and not exclusion. Invite only those members needed to get the job done but try not to exclude persons who need to be or should be present.

Have an agenda printed and distributed ahead of time, including any pertinent materials that need study or consideration prior to the meeting. Always take extra copies of the agenda to the meeting. Organization keeps meetings short and to the point. Distributing the agenda, in advance, allows attendees to bring well thought-out ideas, options and solutions. When the goals for the meeting are defined, the members feel challenged. The motivation will get the issues resolved more quickly.

Show respect for the participants by beginning and ending the meeting on time. Even if some members are late, the meeting begins at the specified time. The standards have been set from the onset.

Bang the gavel only once to open a meeting or adjourn. You are not cracking walnuts. Then open with an orientation comment. Why are you meeting and what actions are desired?

Identify what needs to be done, who will do it and what will happen after it's done. State the action items out loud to the entire team so everyone is on board and knows what is expected. Be certain you embrace another's ideas during the meeting. To be discounted is to be diminished. To be diminished is devastating.

Keep the meeting moving. Don't get side tracked and wander off of the agenda. Avoid sharing personal experiences during the meeting. Finish on time and be sure to thank the participants and give special kudos to those who made presentations or assisted in planning the meeting.

Some additional points that need your attention are:

- Check your posture and don't slouch or slump in your chair.
- Be alert and don't doodle, shuffle papers or fiddle with paper clips, pens or pencils.
- Turn your cell phone off and do not place it or anything else of yours on the conference table such as keys or glasses.
- When you leave the table (meeting or dining) always push in your chair. It leaves a clear path for others.
- If you are in the U.S. or abroad, present your business card before serious discussion begins – never at the end of a meeting.

- When visiting a board meeting, arrive several minutes ahead of time and don't take the first seat available. You will be directed to sit in a specific place. Seats to the right and left of the Chair are for honored guests. The hierarchy of seating goes from left to right. The most coveted seat is to the immediate left of the most influential person at the meeting.

- Give attendees your business card. Place business cards you receive on the table in front of you. It helps keep the names, faces and positions straight. Often, pre-printed tent cards will be placed in advance, for seating and recognition purposes by a thoughtful meeting Chair.

- Remember the 5 P's – Prior Planning Prevents Poor Performance. Read the agenda in advance. Make notes and prepare questions you have noted or comments you wish to make.

- Leave your briefcase in the office. Carry only a portfolio or laptop. Never open a briefcase on a desk or a conference table.

- Ask questions when you don't understand, but don't use the meeting as a forum to promote yourself. Keep your comments concise and relevant to the discussion.

- Don't interrupt or talk over the other participants.

- Pick up all your papers at the end of the meeting and place trash in the waste receptacle.

- Thank the Chair and shake hands as you leave. Also shake the hands of others present if you are from outside the company.

- Hand-write a note of thanks to the person who invited you to attend the meeting, to the Chair and to any persons with whom you hope to work in the future.

- **Be a considerate meeting Chair.** Don't schedule a meeting on Friday afternoon or on the eve of a religious holiday. Try to schedule meetings first thing in the morning when participants are fresh and at their best, and not at the end of a long day.

- Always shake hands with the participants as they depart.

- Distribute the minutes within 48 hours after the meeting.

- Finally. Don't forget a good pen and your breath mints!!!!

# Meeting Planning

Have you been in meetings or training sessions where those in attendance, including yourself, had to fight to stay awake?

If you are responsible for planning or facilitating a meeting for your organization, be sure you lead-off with a dynamic speaker. One who begins with a provocative, challenging premise. Be certain the subject ties in closely with the overall meeting theme.

Your objective, no matter what means you use to achieve it, is to capture your groups' attention and keep it. Begin by setting the mood and the pace of the meeting to establish momentum and assure active participation.

Since a large group can often be unwieldy and often restrict effective participation, consider breaking it into smaller units.

These splinter or "breakout" groups should consist of six to ten members and have an appointed leader ideally selected by the members themselves.

A well-planned agenda should be presented matching the members' common interests. Perhaps a series of questions designed for discussion. A quiz, a simple test of the attendees' knowledge is an effective way to enhance participation or introduce a new subject.

Be sure to keep it informal and very simple. The objective is not to test skills or intelligence levels but rather to get your audience involved.

One must be very careful not to hold anyone up to ridicule or embarrassment for giving a "wrong" answer.

Keep it short with a definite time limit but be aware that some do not read as fast as others and also allow for discussion of differences of opinion.

Another good device for participation is a workshop session. Present a typical problem one may encounter in an everyday employment situation and encourage the attendees to work together toward a solution.

In utilizing the quiz or workshop format, don't over do it. One or two quizzes and a single workshop during the entire meeting are certainly sufficient. You don't want to risk your grand ideas wearing thin or becoming boring.

Most meeting participants enjoy role-playing. This is an effective way to portray some key points and most lessons are learned quickly. The skit or role-playing exercise can include some classical blunders with the objective illustrating to the group how-not-to-do-it and, of course, the how-to-do-it correctly message is the ultimate goal.

Many of these amateur dramatic presentations evolve into a frantic comedy routine with the message obscured and ultimately lost in a barrage of unsolicited and unwanted laughter from the audience.

Your job as the facilitator is to maintain control. Remain aware and be sensitive to the participants' feelings and assure them the respect they are entitled to be shown.

If the humor flows naturally from the situation, spontaneous laughter is far more rewarding than attempting to entertain an audience with home spun humor. It may not be quite as hilarious at the meeting as it seemed in your mind's eye prior to the actual delivery in front of everyone.

Your power point presentations also may be dotted with humorous caricatures and cartoons, which are funny but never insulting or directed at any individual personality. Being humiliated in front of one's peers effects everyone present and is disastrous.

Meetings should not be a waste of time, nor should they be filled with so much entertainment, the attendees feel they have been to a commercial comedy club. The message and/or learning experience is primary and the focus should never be undermined.

By adding novelty gadgets, such as clappers or promotional items are often welcome additions which add an element of surprise to what could otherwise be a dull ho-hum event.

Your meetings will be productive as well as memorable if they are well-planned and proper consideration is given to the details and attendee comfort.

Arrange your meeting at a convenient time and location. Never schedule it before a holiday or just after one due to the workload holiday closings usually cause.

Consider the environment. Be aware of not inviting too many people for too small a space. Are washrooms convenient? Is food service efficient? Arrange the room to accommodate your program – round tables for small break-outs, herringbone or classroom configurations for audio-visual presentations. Make sure your electrical components are in good working order with back-up available.

Don't forget water, writing space, paper, pens and comfortable chairs. Sitting in a straight backed hard chair will cause a major loss of attention very quickly especially if the meeting isn't action-packed. Sporting events are the exception.

Respect your audience and its needs, plan ahead, move ahead and adjourn ASAP.

# Get Opinions

"Don't say yes until I finish talking," said a high powered executive from California. Unfortunately, many an employee thinks the best way to get ahead is to always agree with management. These individuals have gained the reputation and notable title of "Yes Man or Woman."

If associates feel free to question a manager's point of view and also make alternative suggestions, you will have found an excellent manager and a good leader.

When one considers five or six possible answers to a problem, the right solution is more apt to be found than if only one or two are up for discussion. It is very difficult, almost next to impossible, for one person to think of everything and brainstorming is a necessity to facilitate making the best decisions. Those who vacillate seldom succeed or win the solid respect of others.

Certainly it isn't very flattering when those around you disagree with you, especially if you have given your idea considerable thought.

"I want people around me who will tell me the truth as they see it," President Harry Truman once said," You can't operate if you have those around you who put you on a pedestal and tell you everything you do is right."

Vanity has no place with the intelligent leader who recognizes the danger of personal reaction and deliberately sets it aside. Opposing views are a must to cut down on mistakes before they are made as well as to correct past errors.

It is best to remember that our judgment can be no better than our information. The more you listen and ask questions the more stimulation and accuracy will find their way into the decision making process. Also take into consideration that body language often speaks louder than words.

Some personalities need encouragement to allow them to speak their minds. Show them your sincerity by addressing the importance of their contribution. Hear them out when they do have something to say and respect their ideas even if you don't agree with them. Before you form your opinion, ask for theirs. Don't take personal offense or become argumentative due to differing points of view. Show, in your attitude and actions, that you value and appreciate the person who speaks up. Don't hesitate to ask questions or pretend to know all the answers. Be aggressive in gathering valuable information. Don't make excuses for past errors. Making excuses switches the focus. The sight of the original goal is lost. Accept responsibility and empower yourself.

When you let people express their opinions, it doesn't reduce your authority. Neither does it keep you from insisting on 100% support once a final decision has been made. It simply means you are willing to listen and are appreciative of everyone's thoughts and ideas to help reach the best answers.

*The most important thing in communications*
*is to hear what isn't being said.*
Peter F. Drucker

# ELECTRONIC ETIQUETTE:
# BUSINESS – NOT SOCIAL

# Telephone Etiquette

*If you just communicate, you can get by.*
*But if you skillfully communicate, you can work miracles.*

Jim Rohn

Every time the phone rings, your business is on the line. If the telephone is out of service, for even a few hours, frustration sets in. Can you imagine trying to conduct business today without ever using the telephone? Client, attorney, personal, every call is important and costs your company time and money or conversely makes your company profitable.

The telephone is actually the most important piece of equipment in your office. It is more important than the pencil, pen, or computer. You depend on it everyday. How every call is handled will be a great determinant in your level of success.

While teleconferencing and interfacing have become by-words in this high-tech world, a smile still works wonders. Your smile travels over the telephone wire and so does your attitude and energy. Make certain the caller hears a vibrant engaged business person, a professional.

Try this little experiment; without smiling say out loud, "good morning, this is Jack Brown speaking or good morning, this is Jack Brown." Now, say exactly the same thing and smile when you say it. Go ahead-try it-right now – I'll wait.

There! You see! It does sound different doesn't it? Personally, before I ever answer the phone, I glance at the clock or my watch, to check if it is morning or afternoon, and smile as I answer the call, in my office or from my cell phone. It doesn't matter where I am, but how I sound does matter.

The telephone is the most image sensitive tool there is. If you are tired, irritated, in a hurry, inattentive, bored, breathless or half asleep, your caller will definitely get the message. If you are eating, chewing gum or just been to the dentist, your phone also lets your caller hear the change in your voice. Can you imagine the person with a pierced tongue trying to sound professional?

Very often, a caller will start talking when you answer, as though you are supposed to know who it is. It's as though she feels you would know her by the sound of her voice. You never receive other calls. Or, perhaps she will say, "This is Mary." Mary who? Mary is a common name and you just may know 10 others. It's not about you. Identify yourself as a courtesy to the person you called.

Return calls even if it is difficult at times. It is not the callers' fault you have had a bad day, are on vacation, have a full schedule, in a meeting that seemed to last forever, have a plane to catch or a sick child at home.

You may look great, very professional, but how do you sound? Do you bark your name like a drill sergeant? Do you answer with your first and last name after your initial greeting? You should.

Have you ever listened to your voice? Does your voice mail message sound the way you would like to sound? A good communicator does not speak in monotone. Slang such as "bye-bye," "see you later," "catch you later," "so long" or any number of unprofessional utterances are strictly taboo.

If you are an excellent communicator, the impression you project is usually that of a very attractive person, even if you have never seen the caller. On the other hand, a terrible communicator, also unseen, is imagined as a ditz. When you do meet, you are often quite surprised by the appearance of the person you have spoken with so often and pictured in your mind. I have to laugh because, I am often imagined as much younger then I am, which I may say, is not all that bad.

Your basic voice mail message should never say you are away from your desk or on another line. Don't insult the caller's intelligence. He knows that. If you were available, you would have answered the phone.

Instead, be honest, "you have reached the voice mail of Melodie Murphy." You might then continue with "Please leave your message, your phone number, and the best time to reach you. Thank you."

So much money, millions of dollars, has been lost by playing telephone tag, the buyer not reaching the seller and vice-versa.

When you are the caller and leave a message, always say your number twice. Invariably, one digit garbled or deleted will frustrate the person called. Even if you think the person you called knows your number. Leave it anyway for convenience and consideration.

It is very important for you to leave the time of day when you can be reached. This avoids telephone tag and saves time and money. When the response is received, the caller will have the information you need already for you.

Your recorded message should not be cute or cool. These messages do not work well in business, even on your cell phone. Please, no background music, spiritual bells or chimes and no jokes. Never leave a religious message on a business phone and avoid clichés', such as "Have a nice day."

Don't hang up on business. Always let the other person hang up first. Don't assume the call is finished. So much business has been lost in the after thought.

No commercials please. Avoid lengthy advertisements or commercials on your voice-mail. Your caller merely wants to leave a message, and the callers' time is valuable. Offer another line to hear about your company.

Are you on vacation, had surgery, on sick leave, not in yet, on a business trip or heaven forbid, in the washroom? It is no one's business what is keeping you out of the office. On your voice mail message, just announce the date you will be available, even if its three months from now.

If another person answers your phone in your absence, think about how the message comes across. If you are "not in yet," what message does that send? Are you constantly late, playing golf, having a manicure, sleeping late or whatever the caller's imagination can conjure up? The fact that your day began with a 6 a.m. meeting is of no concern to the caller. The damage to your image has been done.

Another business phone tip for today is to think before you speak, even to a recording. Prepare your personal voice mail message in advance and also when making a call, just in case you will need it, if the person called is not available, don't just wing it. A message planned in advance is good insurance that there will be fewer "ah's" and "um's." You will get to the point and state your reasons for calling very successfully. You will sound professional with excellent communication skills. There might just be a "miracle" hidden in the call somewhere.

# Telephone Personality

A warm friendly personality is a power magnet. Most of us are naturally drawn to a person who is cheerful and congenial.

Do you answer your phone with a one-two punch? I have heard many men, and yes, women too, bark their names as though they were actually irritated by the interruption. The expression, "This would be a nice place to work accept for the customers," seems to be the attitude du jour in many offices.

You must realize the caller "sees" us in his mind's eye. What we say is important but how we say it means even more. When you answer the phone, allow your full personality to shine.

I had a friend, who taught me a very valuable lesson years ago. She was blind. One day when I stopped by for a visit and she said," Oh, I'm so glad you're here. You look very pretty today." I smiled and asked "how would you know how I look?" She answered, "Because I can hear it." Ever since that day, I've tried to send the message of someone who really cares when I answer the phone. I want to "look good" when the caller hears me.

I guess you could say I have a determined approach to achieve a desired goal. Knowing my company is professional in the service we provide is not enough. We must deliver that message at every opportunity.

It is the same for any company. You can't just talk the talk about how well you fill the needs of your customers. You must walk the walk, if they are going to believe in you.

Some are known for answering the phone in a semi-shout, as though they are speaking to someone across a large room. I'm quite aware that for those who answer a large number of calls, sometimes it gets exasperating but don't let it show in your voice.

With the computer being an excellent form of communication and the fingers adept at creating speedy communications, sometimes we talk as fast as our fingers move. Video games have produced a generation of quick-think, reaction and action. Cell phones and text messaging also have given thumbs great dexterity training. But it is amazing that some callers talk so fast you can't keep up. Sometimes you must play a voice mail message over three or four times to get what the caller wants you to know and be able to write down the phone number accurately.

Animated conversation or vocal variety lifts the spirit. A blah, monotone or agitated voice is not your best choice. You must try a little imaginative spirit expansion. You could practice substituting positive words such as "I'll try," instead of "I can't." Think of all the negative responses you normally give and change them to reflect your positive personality. It will work wonders for you and your spirit will be lifted along with your callers.

Don't get caught answering the phone with a curt "Yes" and then continue to keep a running conversation with someone else near you, while completely ignoring the caller.

Every phone call, every day deserves to hear a pleasant, cheerful, enthusiastic person answer. There is no room for good days and bad days. Even if you handle 99 complaints beautifully, there is not justification for treating the 100th caller rudely.

Enthusiasm energizes everything we do. It definitely helps create a terrific telephone personality. It is said, we are all in sales. Can you imagine professional sales persons lacking enthusiasm for the product or service they represent?

Your telephone personality is very powerful. You have, within your grasp, the opportunity to brighten someone's day by being caring, courteous and sensitive or to drag them down, even irritate them to frustration.

For the very best impression, use a low, calm tone while keeping your enthusiasm alive. Using proper English language and avoiding slang helps create the kind of impression you want. People remember how you have made them feel and your customers are no different. They like to do business with those who respect them, appreciate them and sound like it.

# The Angry Caller

Occasionally, everyone who uses a business telephone has to interact with someone who is angry.

If it is an angry customer or client, you are truly blessed. It is a wonderful opportunity for you to shine as a trained concerned professional and for your company to project the image no amount of advertising dollars can buy. If handled properly the angry caller can become a catalyst for your company, to become known as the company customers rave about and send business too.

Just think for a moment. What if the caller didn't call to vent this displeasure and called all his friends and neighbors instead. He might tell 20 or 30 people about how angry he is about doing business with your rotten company.

How unfair your company is and how dissatisfied he is with your customer no-service, your product and terrible attitude. Usually when one is unhappy the story that's shared seems to generally be embellished with additional negatives.

When this caller retells his dreadful experience, he is actually preventing many prospective customers from doing business with you. In some cases, customers you already have are moved to take their business elsewhere.

Statistics tell us that a satisfied customer will generally tell four or five people about what a pleasure it is to do business with you. Conversely, an angry customer will tell ten to twenty about a negative experience.

The manner in which you handle the situation is extremely important to your bottom line.

Remember your instinctive reaction to someone who is angry or very critical is to respond in kind. Anger begets anger. That's the worst thing you can do. Kindness also begets kindness. You must control your emotions if you have any hope of controlling the situation. Keep your voice calm, speak slowly and be helpful after you have listened.

Yes listen! Think of a mountain of anger which the caller is going to climb. If you interrupt, defend, contradict or become sarcastic, you certainly will push the caller back down the mountain and he will start climbing all over again. If you just listen as he climbs or expresses his anger, it will take approximately 30 to 45 seconds for him to reach the top. You will actually hear when he reaches the top – he stops talking and takes a breath.

Now it's your turn to bring him down the other side of the mountain and keep a customer who is actually a pot of gold. Agree with him without misleading. Empathize and let him know you understand and the anger is justified. It is difficult to be angry with someone who agrees with you. If the fault lies with you or your company, admit it. Anger dissipates and the caller's temperature drops with an honest acknowledgement of error.

Thank the caller for taking the time to call and for bringing the issue to your attention.

Do everything you can to correct the problem immediately. If this is not possible, explain what you are going to do to rectify the situation including bringing it to the attention of management.

If anyone uses foul language along with their anger, calmly remind them that you want to help them. If the language continues, remind them again that you understand their frustration and want to help but you won't be able to do that if they use that type of language to communicate the problem you are trying to solve.

Three times and they are out! You do not have to listen to one who swears at you, calls you names, or is insulting in any manner. Apologize and say you will not be able to help them and hang up. Yes – hang up. After five minutes or so, call the client, announce who you are and that you want to help followed by

"Let's begin again."

Nine times out of ten the caller will be willing to restate the problem in a rational manner and the problem will be resolved.

Never take the anger even if directed at you, personally. Don't try to defend yourself or the company but let that angry caller go ahead and climb that mountain. The situation will be handled, you have retained a good customer, and perhaps changes in company policy may be implemented all because you knew how to handle the angry caller, appreciated him and kept your cool. Your key to that pot of gold.

# E-Mail Etiquette

E lectronic mail (e-mail) has changed the way business is conducted today. More organizations than ever use e-mail to distribute memos, circulate drafts, disseminate directives, transfer official documents, send external correspondence, and support various aspects of their operations. A well-designed and managed e-mail system is an invaluable communication tool which eliminates paperwork and automates many routine office tasks as it expedites business.

Sounds great but the same e-mail system can also cause chaos in the office. Personal use of e-mail, loss of control over official records and important documents, increases in trivial and duplicate messages, and privacy, security and public access may offset the benefits.

Let's keep it simple and look at your basic e-mail etiquette. With help from Priscilla Emery of Enterprise Advisors and several written guidelines such as: Gargano, *Guide to Electronic Communication and Network Etiquette;* Goode and Johnson, *Putting Out the Flames: the Etiquette and Law of E-mail;* Krol, *The Whole Internet Users Guide and Catalog;* and Robinson, *Delivering Electronic Mail,* I offer the following information for your effective e-mail communication and to help eliminate office squabbles.

**Know your audience**

Be aware of the culture and conventions of your e-mail recipients. Communication and especially e-mail conventions may vary between groups. Remember, different users have different levels of experience with technology applications like e-mail. Be patient and supportive with new users. Be sensitive to different verbiage and word usage in other countries. For example, in the UK the word "pants" refers to men's undergarments while "trousers" or "slacks" are just what they sound like.

## Proofread

Spelling and grammar mistakes can be just as distracting in an e-mail message as they are in written communications. Take the time to proofread your messages, especially messages that are used to communicate or document company business. Sometimes just reading the message out loud to yourself first can help ferret out "fuzzy" verbiage and make sure that the message makes sense. If it sounds a little weird to you, your recipient may misinterpret your true intentions when they read it.

## Keep messages brief and to the point

Make your messages "concise" not cryptic. Shorter paragraphs have more impact and are more likely to be read by busy people. Most people can only grasp a limited number of ideas within a single paragraph, especially on a computer screen.

## Format messages for easy reading

White space enhances the look and clarity of an e-mail message, and a blank line only adds a byte to the message so don't be stingy. Lengthy messages are almost always read in hard copy form and should be prepared accordingly (e.g., with cover sheets, headers, page numbers, and formatting). E-mail is for messaging not long dissertation. I personally don't believe in sending very long messages. If the message is really a lengthy memo or report, create a separate attachment and send it that way. If the topic is important you might also consider giving a speech or presentation, on the subject, to the interested parties.

## Don't over-distribute e-mail

Every message you send creates work for someone else who must read, consider, and deal with the message. It may be better to post some messages or large documents on an electronic bulletin board or shared repository in order to reduce the number of copies routed to individual users.

## Respect the privacy rights of others

Don't invade privacy. Don't forward or distribute messages without permission. Don't read other people's mail. If you receive someone else's mail, e.g., because the sender entered a wrong address or you happen upon a PC or terminal someone failed to log-off of, use the same consideration you would with traditional mail. Inform the appropriate party, and see that the mail is returned.

## Be aware of differences across e-mail systems

Others may not have the same e-mail features or capabilities you have, in which case, avoid special control characters like bold, underline, and special fonts; even tabs can differ. Be extra careful with graphics.

## Cite the appropriate references and context of a message

Reference any related e-mail message or posting, and the event, topic, or issue that your message refers to, in order to avoid being taken out of context and misinterpreted. Take the time to back up your statements with references to documents or articles just as you would in written material. If a message is referencing an earlier note, include enough of the original message to make the message clear.

## Identify yourself

Especially if you are acting on behalf of an organization or professional association, or if you have relevant background or expertise in a matter, identify your affiliation, title, background, and expertise in your e-mail message. Include your e-mail address in the message and any attachments to it.

## Separate opinion from non-opinion

So that readers do not confuse personal opinion with your company's policy or position, use labels and explanatory notes to distinguish opinion from fact. If necessary, include a brief disclaimer.

## Respect copyright and license agreements

Copyright laws are applicable to e-mail networks. Some software that is available for public retrieval through the Internet requires a valid license from the vendor in order to use it legally. Posting information on networks is similar to publication. Be careful to cite references.

## Label messages that are meant to be humorous, and be careful with sarcasm

Use established conventions or explanatory notes to alert the recipient that a message is meant to be taken humorously. Facial expressions, voice inflection and other cues that help recipients to interpret a message are absent from e-mail. You can't always control when and in what context a message will be read. It might be read at the wrong time or by the wrong party. The reader might not understand your intention. In general, jokes are time wasters – limit them to a core group.

## NEVER send a chain letter

## Avoid sending e-mail in anger or as an emotional response

It is best not to send these kinds of messages over e-mail. Such situations are better worked out in person or in another forum. If you do send such a message, be sure to warn readers of your intent with the use of established conventions or explanatory notes. (These messages are often called "flames.) When it comes to confrontation many people like to use e-mail to lash out because it "feels" anonymous. It's not. What you put in an e-mail can be used in court or to pursue disciplinary action by human resources. If you have a problem with someone it is best to use the phone or face the person and discuss it calmly and rationally.

## Don't be hasty

If a message or posting generates negative feelings, set it aside and reread it later. An immediate response is often a hasty response. Don't rule out the possibility that a misunderstanding or misinterpretation might occur. It is common with e-mail because of the lack of physical cues.

## Avoid putting text in all capital letters

Most users suggest that you avoid putting all text in caps because it may seem angry, harsh or that you are shouting. Uppercase text is often interpreted as having extra emphasis. Conversely, all lower case letters gives the impression of sloppiness.

## Be careful what you say about yourself and others

As a general rule of thumb, don't commit anything to e-mail that you wouldn't want to become public knowledge. Think twice before posting personal information about yourself or others. There is always the chance that a message could end up in someone else's hands. Be aware that e-mail messages are often retained on system backup tapes and disks in central computing facilities after they are deleted from the mail system.

## Don't be fooled by the illusion of privacy

Assume that your message could be around for a long time. It is easy to copy, store (electronically or in hard copy), resurrect, and forward anything you write in e-mail.

## Don't send abusive, harassing, or bigoted messages

This is inappropriate and counterproductive for obvious reasons and reflects badly on the individual and the entire organization. Even on wide area networks, e-mail can usually be traced to the originating machine and user. Systems on the Internet are actually liable for the misdeeds of their users.

## Reread your mail for content and tone before you send it

On many systems, once you send a message you are committed to it, and cannot retract it.

## Try to keep messages to a single subject and use subject entries

The subject line of an e-mail message serves a number of important purposes: (1) it enables busy people to discern the subject of a message and when it must be read; (2) it is used to index the message in mailboxes and file folders; (3) it may be used to identify what messages are "records" and need to be transferred to a central record keeping system at your company.

**Only post messages when they are relevant**

**Don't make messages "urgent" when they don't need to be**

Most of us learned the lesson of "the boy who cried wolf" quite some time ago. In today's world, this lesson rings true for the misuse of priority mail notices. These notices will soon become meaningless with overuse.

**Respond to e-mails in a timely fashion**

E-mail inboxes can become as piled up with all kinds of messages and it can be tempting to ignore them but it is non-professional and discourteous when you receive a business communication and do not respond to any action items or requests for information within 24 hours. Of course, not every e-mail requires an answer. But you have to actually read your mail in order to know that.

Here are some strategies for speeding up the process of getting through your e-mail.

- Do e-mail triage – once in the morning and once in the afternoon.
- Set up e-mail folders to manage mail
- By Topic
- By Urgency
- Sort by Sender and Date
- Deal with the message once – like paper – respond, file or discard.
- Subscribe to mailing lists sparingly. If you must subscribe, send to separate personal (junk) e-mail address.
- Auto send routine messages to a specific folder in your e-mail Inbox if possible.
- Try to have a business account and a personal account
- Use the Right Tool for the job
- Don't use your Inbox as a Tickler File

- Use Task Manager or Calendar to Manage Things to Do and Appointments
- Use Advanced Calendaring features to set up meetings instead of sending out large distribution lists and chasing people

## Bottom line

- E-mail is viewed as a serious communication vehicle
- How quickly you respond (or don't respond) to e-mail sends a message to colleagues and associates about how you manage your business and your activities overall.
- Don't forget spelling, grammar and punctuation.
- If a message is going to be more than two or three paragraphs create a document and attach.
- Never use all caps for any communication – even if you are angry.
- Don't let e-mail control you – set aside the time, deal with the issues and then move on.

# DINING SKILLS

# Using Fingers, Forks
# or Chopsticks

It may sound simple when I say that your flatware or eating utensils are not weapons. Simple to you, yes, but it is amazing how many sophisticated, educated and seemingly well-mannered individuals are unaware, oblivious or have merely forgotten the proper use of knives, forks, spoons and chopsticks.

As silent as the rituals of dining may be, even when your voice is still you are communicating. The improper use of your dining services definitely sends the wrong message.

It is timely for us to review the use of our fingers, forks and one of the most often used eating utensils in the world – chopsticks. By the way, as a point of information, fingers are the *most* used.

Don't take food from a serving plate or bowl with your own chopsticks. It's the same as double dipping in the U.S.A. and a definite No-No. Another set should be provided for service, or in some cases a spoon will be offered. If neither one is provided, turn your chopsticks upside down to use the clean wide ends to serve yourself. Always place your chopsticks side by side on the plate or table and avoid crossing them.

Practice using chopsticks and have some fun while at it. You will learn quickly if you try to use your chopsticks to eat popcorn one piece at a time. No cheating.

In the United States, we do use our fingers to eat certain foods: chips and dip immediately come to mind along with hors d' oeuvres, canapés, and crudités.

Hors d' oeuvres are finger foods served prior to a meal. They are generally eaten while standing, having a cocktail and over conversation. A canapé is food served on a crust-less piece of bread. Crudités are raw vegetables often served with a flavored dip. Of course, we cannot forget popcorn. We do however often forget that popcorn is a finger food not meant to be eaten by the handful.

On the other hand (no pun intended) the preferred utensils in some countries are the fingers. Eskimos, Saudis and those from India much prefer fingers to forks. In these cultures, the hands are washed before and after eating.

Fingers and chopsticks are most used throughout the world. In Japan, chopsticks or hashi (HAH-SHE) are made of wood. Since chopsticks are the eating utensils of choice for most Asians, it is best to learn how to use them correctly if you are serious about becoming a successful executive in today's global community.

I have seen young business people drinking cocktails with the plastic stirring mixer still in the glass. I've also witnessed these people's coffee being drunk with the spoon left in the cup. I do fear for safety. I'm so afraid they will lose an eye. Please remember to remove these encumbrances before drinking from a glass or cup.

Also, on the no-no list is the use of knife and/or fork as a pointer. When dining, or at anytime for that matter, a knife or fork should never be waved around in conversation or pointed at anyone or anything. A used utensil should never be placed back on the table. Once it has been used for any purpose it is placed on a plate or saucer.

Your dinner knife is placed at the top of the plate with the blade facing you. It is a sign of peace. If the blade faces out, it could conceivably be used as a weapon. This holds especially true of a steak knife, which is very sharp.

You can always recognize an American, in any country; just by the way she holds her fork. However, more Americans are eating in the Continental or European style than ever before. Why? It's easier, quieter and accepted worldwide. Americans are the only people who eat like we do. If you drop your silver or your napkin on the floor, leave it. Quietly signal your server to bring a replacement. Crawling around under the table is not good form.

Your soup spoon, the one shaped like a bowl, is held just like a pencil except horizontal, rather than perpendicular. Soup is spooned away from you (as the ships go out to sea) and the bottom of the spoon may touch the opposite side of the bowl to catch any drips before you bring the soup to your mouth or dribble on our tie.

The cup or soup bowl may be tipped away from you, not toward you, to help retrieve the last spoonful or two. If you have ordered a cup of soup, never leave the spoon in the cup – or in a cup of coffee, for that matter. The spoon, when not in use, should be placed on the plate underneath and beside the cup or bowl.

Hot or cold soups should be eaten with a spoon. However you may drink a clear soup or broth from a cup, if it has handles, just as you would a cup of coffee. Rarely is a clear soup served, but occasionally you might enjoy a bouillon or consommé. Sip it, don't chug it. And never blow on any soup to cool it. It will cool by itself. Be patient.

Please don't spit seeds, pits and tiny unwanted surprises into your napkin. They should come out the way they went in. Gently spit them into your spoon or onto your fork and place them on the side of your plate without fanfare. Be discreet, if possible.

Very often the way you hold your fork and knife will put you at a shameful disadvantage. Let's build confidence and refinement so you will feel comfortable dining anyplace in the world.

# Business Lunch

You have called a client and suggested meeting for lunch. Wonderful! Where? If you are a considerate host you would select the restaurant based on the location closest to the clients' home or business. You would also take into consideration the clients' business. For example, if he is blue collar, you wouldn't invite him to lunch at "The Ritz." Is the lunch to be a quick casual get-together or is heavy duty business the object? If serious business is going to be discussed, a casual, noisy, informal eatery is not the best choice. Select a place which is more suited to serious discussion and perhaps a bit more upscale.

When you arrive at the restaurant, which should be before your guest or guests, give your credit card to the maitre d' or the person seating you. This will leave no doubt or confusion as to who is paying the check.

Always opt for an out of the way table rather than a booth. You have heard conversations behind you when you have been sitting in a booth. To eliminate your private business discussion being overheard, the table is your best choice.

Wait for your guest to arrive before being seated. This allows you to offer her the seat of her choice. Don't order something to drink while you are waiting. It will make your guest feel as if she was late even if she is not.

After you are seated, never put anything on the table – no car keys, glasses, cell phones, handbags, papers, or folders. Also keep books, computers and large folders, off the table. Focus on the other person and don't be pre-occupied with objects. Later on, if you must write something, use a small card or a note pad.

A woman should avoid walking through a restaurant with a glass in her hand – no drink, even if it is water. The wait staff is to bring the drink to the table. The beverage might spill, the glass is wet, and a drink in the hand is not a plus for a women's appearance.

When attending an event, from a gala to a business lunch, give up the bottle. If you feel you must have beer, order it in a glass. Do not walk around with a bottle in your hand, drink out of a beer bottle or set a beer bottle on the table. It is much better to avoid alcohol altogether. However, a glass of wine is totally acceptable, or perhaps a glass of tonic with lime. Leave the vodka for another time. Remember, we are talking about a business lunch or dinner. I've said many times that the rules for social behavior and business protocol are different. So please keep this in mind. You must know the difference to make a difference.

When you enter your chair, enter and exit from the right. You will avoid bumping into each other. In an upscale restaurant, the wait person will not take your order until you close the menu. Silent codes are observed and followed by most trained wait staff.

Dining skills are extremely important in the competitive business arena.

We have touched today on the beginning of the meal. There is much more ahead about the meal itself.

# In-Home Dining
## with Upper Management

I once heard about a formal dinner in the home of a chief executive officer where the manners exhibited by even senior managers was so appalling, the host made etiquette classes mandatory for all of the executives in his company.

Hard to believe? It shouldn't be, because it is not unusual. Company CEOs have found etiquette training is a worthwhile investment even for themselves. In many cases, people skills are more important than technical skills. Today's CEOs are well aware that business has been lost due to social ineptitude of younger managers, and there is a definite decline in human interaction due to the high-tech workplace.

You may be right in making your point, but if you are rude, vulgar, ostentatious, or demeaning when presenting your opinion, you are not right but very, very wrong. Skills that you think you have are often the very skills you do not have, and you don't even know it.

Whether it is a formal dinner, or a business lunch, many of the nuances of blunder-free dining are appropriate and expected. A business lunch or dinner is not about eating. It is about business and the professional image you project.

If you are the host, you want your guests to feel comfortable, and the time spent with you is a worthwhile investment. You want to provide an enjoyable atmosphere and accomplish business at the same time for a win-win event.

A business meal is not a time for the scoop and shovel crowd to shine. Rather, it is a time to easily communicate your social acumen and exhibit your professional presence.

Approximately 90 percent of all high-level executives are taken to lunch or dinner before they are hired. Not because the would-be employer thinks they are hungry. It is to test social skills, communication skills and, yes, table manners to see whether or not the future manager or executive will be able to represent the company at social events and business meals.

Often, the spouse is included in the pre-hire process. I know of one example when the wife of a candidate arrived for lunch wearing her jogging suit. Right then and there, the interview process ceased.

It is important to remember that a spouse is a partner. Your spouse can be a benefit or a stumbling block. When a spouse is asked to join you at an important business event, it is your responsibility to make certain you explain expectations and who's who on the guest list.

When you are dining at your employer's home and you enjoy mint jelly with lamb, or applesauce with pork, and it hasn't been served, don't ask for it. Your request could be embarrassing because the item was forgotten or unavailable.

Mentioning diets, cholesterol content, or the fact that you never touch fried foods, especially if they're on the menu, can make your host and others at the table very uncomfortable. To assure you won't be invited again, try talking about your weight-loss, fiber content or cancer-fighting vegetables. Remind everyone to drink at least eight glasses of water every day, and punctuate your lecture by making everyone feel less than perfect. That should do it!

As an invited guest, it is customary to bring a small gift. Do not bring flowers, which must be immediately arranged. Do not bring wine you expect to be opened and shared. Do not bring candy, which tempts a dieter or, even worse, a diabetic. Small books, a plant, or a flower arrangement in a decorative container are very appropriate gifts. You could also select a good bottle of wine and present it unchilled to be enjoyed at another time.

Although it is necessary to arrive early for a business event, it is not considered good form to arrive early at a private home. If you have had an unavoidable problem, call ahead and let the host know you will be late.

Always carry a good supply of business cards. Try never to be without them, even socially. An occasion may arise when you'll be glad you carried your cards. Be discreet, however, and careful in a private home. If business cards are exchanged, try to find a private spot, perhaps a hallway. Don't ever produce a business card at a private luncheon or dinner in the presence of others. This was also addressed in the chapter about business cards.

No peeking! As a guest in anyone's home, especially that of your boss, don't wander from room to room taking yourself on an unauthorized tour. Avoid peeking into the medicine cabinet or behind closed doors. You may just inadvertently wake the baby or let the dog out.

If you are hosting an event, and it is getting late, and you as the host, want your guest to make their exit gracefully here is a little hint. Casually walk toward the door and take your place. As your guests stop by to talk with you, they will automatically take their leave. It is a gesture that guides the subconscious mind very effectively.

A few extra suggestions you may find helpful are actually reminders:

- Remember to pass the salt and pepper together. Think of them as a bride and groom. They should never be separated.
- When passing food, always pass to the right around the table. Keep foods moving in the same direction.
- Your bread plate is on the left; your liquids are always on the right. Sometimes it does get confusing.
- Never put a used utensil on the table. Put it on the plate, saucer, or bread plate. Never use it to point or wave it in the air.
- Don't begin to eat anything until the host has begun to eat.
- Open your napkin under the table and place it in your lap, with the fold facing you. Never under your chin, unless you are younger than five years old.
- No elbows on the table, please, and take small bites so you can participate in table conversation without talking with food in your mouth.
- The expression "turning the tables" comes from the practice of talking to the person on your right and then on your left. Don't focus your attention on one person, especially your spouse, but "turn the tables" and include as many guests as possible in the conversation.

Finally, remember there is a distinction between your business life and your personal life. When you treat colleagues as friends and family, it often has a disastrous effect. Don't allow the invitation to dinner at the bosses' home destroy the sense of boundaries which characterizes professional behavior. It's just a friendly dinner. Oh, no it isn't. Remember, your boss also fires people.

When engaged in conversation, after a glass of wine or two, be careful not to reveal something too personal about yourself. Don't reveal too much because you will definitely come to regret it.

Don't forget to send your handwritten thank you note, thanking the host and hostess for your invitation. Never say, "Thank you for having me." They didn't have you! They had mashed potatoes and roasted chicken. Only cannibals have you!

# Holiday Office Party

Whoa! Hold on a minute! Bells and whistles are going off as the office Holiday party gets underway. What in the world are you thinking? This is a business office party or holiday dinner. It is not your social event of the year or your perfect dinner date.

Let's regroup and take a look at this holiday event for what it really is. We must get some of the protocols straight concerning behavior, what to wear, what to eat, and what to do or not do.

I have a tendency to tell it like it is without much sugar coating. It is my mission to tell you that most of the younger inexperienced set of business people doesn't seem to have a clue about this traditional event.

First of all – what is it and why are you there? What are the risks and the benefits?

The holiday business party is the perfect time for the business to shine, show off and entertain clients, VIPs, associates, staff and yes, potential clients. It is also a time when decorations are festive and beautiful. An atmosphere of jovial camaraderie is evident and most of all, it is a time to say "thank you" and show appreciation in the spirit of the season of giving and hospitality.

It is not about you. It is about the business. It is not a personal social event and those attending are not your friends. They are business associates and acquaintances. Get over yourself.

Why are you there? You were invited by the business host because you are being thanked for your association during the year – for your business, your help, your public relations, your hard work, team effort and any contribution you have made or your host thinks you have made. The second reason you may be there is because the host thinks you have something to contribute

146

either now or in the future. In either case, it is time for you to sing for your supper.

You are not going clubbing and neither is it a personal social invitation, so be certain you dress appropriately. Men may wear a festive tie (in the spirit of the season), if it is understated and doesn't light up, or curl up and wave. Women should forget the strapless, sleeveless dresses and cleavage display. The only thing you are displaying is your poor judgment. Don't appear with bare legs and strappy glitzy shoes. This is not the time or place to bare all.

It is however, the perfect time for any attendee to be the professional business person and interact with the guests, meet and greet, make introductions, assist with the flow, compliment, appreciate and be a contributor to the success of the event. Show your good taste and respect by the choice of your apparel and your professional abilities, especially your communication skills, if you want to be working for the company next year.

Your boss is there and members of upper management along with their spouses. Make an excellent impression and at the same time enjoy yourself as you circulate. Don't spend too much time in one place and remember to arrive a little late and exit early.

Try not to invade another person's space by standing too close and watch the volume of your voice. Be conscious of your language and don't be too loud or become obnoxious. Because there is an open bar, does not give you license to over indulge. The food is presented beautifully and with great care. Please help yourself to a sampling. Don't stuff your face, talk with food in your mouth, or stand in front of the food display and chat so others can't get to the chocolate dipped strawberries. Never put your drink glass down on the food table, especially if your glass is empty. There are bus tables for that purpose. Carry your drink in your left hand so your right hand is always free, dry and ready for the handshake – the ultimate greeting.

The overfriendly, cheery holiday season doesn't give you an excuse for unlimited huggy-bear, kissie face. A sprig of mistletoe doesn't belong in the office. Once again, you and your conduct are being observed by those who hold the key to your career advancement in their hands.

If your spouse is invited, remember that your spouse is also your business partner. Be certain you review expectations ahead of time, who's who on the guest list and acknowledge your host. Don't forget to send a personalized handwritten thank you note for being invited to this special event.

Smile! Enjoy! Be happy, alert and aware that that the office holiday tradition is strictly business – in disguise.

# *Buffet Dining*

The Chairman of the Board of a well-known bank recently asked me to address an issue of concern to him. The subject is dining skills especially at a buffet.

I didn't realize how urgent and important this issue is until I recently attended a major event where a buffet meal was served and I was horrified – really shocked by the conduct of most of the attendees.

Some examples of gross behavior which are at the top of the "Never Do" list are shared with you in an attempt to bring this unacceptable behavior to your attention. Each of the following examples was observed by me at just one event, but is repeated time and again on many occasions.

When the invitation to dinner was announced by the Master of Ceremonies, you would have thought the flood gates opened as a sea of humanity rushed en masse toward the food stations. I actually thought people were going to trample each other as they pushed and shoved to get in line. It was, what appeared to be, a group heading for food supplies after a national disaster. There was very little restraint visible to this observer.

For their own protection, some guests remained at their table rather than risk being injured in the rush – or so I thought. I later found they had given orders to their table-mates to bring back several orders of food. That would be a no-no unless one was assisting the disabled.

As I took my life in my hands and joined the hordes, I found myself in a lengthy queue which became even longer because dozens in front of me invited their friends and neighbors to cut in line.

Much to my dismay, I saw guests picking up food from the serving table and actually standing, even walking and eating right there. Crumbs were falling from their mouths and back onto the table and into the food display. Please dear readers, NEVER eat anything while at the buffet or while standing in line.

My next shock came when I saw dirty drink glasses and wet paper napkins placed on the buffet table, in the middle and around the food arrangements. I thought I was in a different world and I certainly was. I went to a server standing nearby and asked him to remove the dirty drink glasses. He hastened to oblige with apologies flowing. He also stated, "It happens all the time. People today only think of themselves."

It is highly improper to carry a drink while in a buffet line. Do I actually have to say don't put anything used on a buffet table where food is being presented and served?

I watched a man take a plate and shove it into some chips using it as a shovel so the plate was piled high. Speaking of piled high, the guests piled their plates so high with food; they had to juggle with two hands to carry it all back to the table seating. You would have thought they hadn't eaten for days and this was the only opportunity.

Please take a petite sampling of the food selections and after everyone has been served, it is permissible to return for a second helping.

Very often, as was the case at this event, three tables are set for appetizers, entrée and dessert. Many people were eating the first course while in line approaching the table for the next course or putting all the courses, even dessert, on one plate. Dirty plates ended up on the buffet table along with clean plates to be used for the current offering.

An errant meatball crossed my path and I knew in a flash things were out of control. Strewn among the fabulous jewelry were vestiges of toast points. It was also obvious that the proceeding cocktail hour had fatigued a few who stood sans shoes as they invited their friends to join them in line.

I re-read the invitation to this clearly business event, which some chose to ignore. The purpose of the affair was business, but people brought uninvited children and strollers to impose on the guests at this clearly adult function.

This event was just one occasion but unfortunately, the scene is repeated at weddings, luncheons and numerous special events. The object of the buffet service is to serve many people in a rather short period of time as efficiently and gracefully as possible.

If you are responsible for a function where buffet service is the main source for food, there are a few protocols, in addition to the ones mentioned, which must be observed.

Tables should be numbered and guests invited to partake in groups by the room captain or other appointee. Guests seated at the head table or at reserved tables such as major sponsors or honorees are served first. Also, persons with disabilities should be considered and accommodated.

Insure the stations are two sided to help with the traffic flow and avoid congestion and long lines.

For those who don't get the message about not carrying drinks, place an easily bussed service tray near the buffet line on which to place used glasses, napkins, paper umbrellas and tooth picks.

The way to avoid self-service shoveling is to have each station staffed. This makes for a more efficient and elegant service.

Eat a little something before you attend and remember an open bar is not an invitation to over-indulge.

Your hosts have provided a lovely event which your behavior can turn into a very unpleasant occasion. Don't think your conduct is not being observed. Remember your thank-you note and, to turn a phrase, "You are how and what you eat."

# Finger Bowl Foibles

The savvy executive often is invited to diplomatic or formal dinners both here in the United States and abroad. As expected, these dinners are longer with more courses served and they usually are also more formal in service.

The use of the finger bowl is often the most confusing at a fine dinner. When the waiter arrives with a large plate holding a doily, a finger bowl and a large fork and spoon, often the guest looks nonplused.

If ever you are seated at dinner, you needn't go blank if you are confused or just absolutely do not know what to do next. Most of the well-known manners mavens offer the same advice and that is to look around to see how others are coping with the same accoutrements. When in Rome, do as the Romans do or so the saying goes. You will probably notice other guests looking at you to see what you are going to do because they don't have a clue either.

Barbara to the rescue! If you are faced with the finger bowl dilemma just relax. From now on, you will know what to do when others don't. You will have the key.

When the finger bowl arrives, after dinner and before the dessert course, take the silver pieces (fork and spoon) and place them on either side of the plate – fork left – spoon right. Then pick up the doily and finger bowl and place them both to upper-left side, and the large plate underneath will now be ready to receive the dessert.

We have an exception to the rule oft times quoted – "solids on the left-liquids on the right." The finger bowl is not to be drunk therefore it is considered in the solid category. No wonder you're confused.

151

Tom Selleck was on the David Letterman show and told everyone that when he was invited to a Margaret Thatcher dinner, he first thought the finger bowl, with its green garnish, was a strange after-dinner soup. He wasn't the only one. Eleanor Roosevelt, once observed an inexperienced guest pick up his finger bowl and drink its contents. She thoughtfully spared his feelings by drinking hers.

Maxine Cheshire, writing in *The Washington Post*, tells us of a dinner at the White House hosted by President Lyndon and Lady Bird Johnson. Joan Crawford, the movie star, and Cathy Douglas, then the 23-year-old bride of the late Justice William O. Douglas were seated on either side of the presidential assistant, Joe Califano. Ms. Crawford spent the entire dinner disparaging Cathy Douglas' background, manners and devotion to the environment. Interior Secretary Stewart Udall tried to quiet the famous Mother Dearest to no avail.

Cheshire wrote: "When finger bowls were set before each guest, she (Ms. Crawford) rose half-way out of her chair, leaned across Mr. Califano and snatched doily and all from in front of Mrs. Douglas and deposited them where they should be. The implication was quite plain that a girl of humble origins, dining for the first time in such splendor, would not know what to do with a finger bowl unless shown."

Ms. Cheshire added that after that, social opinion swung definitely over to Mrs. Douglas' side and her place in society was guaranteed.

The point of these stories is to affirm that you do not have to be bowled over when the finger bowl is placed in front of you. Your thoughtfulness and consideration are what is noteworthy and poor manners, when observed, become stories never to be forgotten.

# Additional Savvy Dining Skills

*The world was my oyster but I used the wrong fork.*
Oscar Wilde

It seems there is a great deal of confusion about the correct way of eating certain foods and what to do with the myriad pieces of flatware that lie before us. The following suggestions are more than helpful hints. Savvy dining skills play a major role in the business arena today. The top management of many companies takes potential front-line employees to lunch or dinner simply to observe their comfort level. Like it or not, management equates good manners with competence in business and poor manners with incompetence.

In addition to the suggestions, or the gentle way of saying "the absolutes," you might want to consider the following:

Your knife and fork should not be placed on the sides of the plate with the handles touching the table. This reminds us of two oars on a rowboat. It is recommended that you cut your salad with your fork. On some occasions, a salad knife will be placed next to your entrée knife after the salad course this knife will be removed.

When you need to stir sugar into a beverage, especially one with ice, place the tip of your spoon so it touches the bottom of the glass or cup. Gently move the spoon back and forth and the clanking sound of ice hitting glass will be avoided.

I mentioned before, never leave your drink stirrer in your glass or a spoon in your glass or cup while you are drinking anything. You just might lose an eye. Don't leave a soup spoon in a soup cup while talking or when you are finished. Place it on the plate under the cup or bowl.

All those little pieces of paper, sugar envelopes, limes, lemons, toothpicks, cherry stems and paper umbrellas should be placed on the butter plate never on the table. Hopefully, the wait staff will be of service and dispose of them for you. If no service plate is available, kindly ask for one. There is usually a paper napkin available which is only to be used as a last resort.

When drinking a cup of coffee or tea, do not place both of your hands around the bowl of the cup. On a frosty night, while sitting around a bon fire this may feel comfy as it warms your fingers surrounding a mug of hot chocolate, spiced wine or steaming coffee. In a dining room, however, bring the cup to your lips using the handle only. It's not freezing in the room nor is the cup so heavy you need both hands to hold it.

When eating with chopsticks use the narrow end for securing the food and hold the sticks a little higher than midway. Do not use the chop sticks as drumsticks or rub them together. They are not meant to be musical instruments. Make certain the chop sticks are even and hold the bottom stick, the stick that doesn't move, in the hollow of your thumb with it resting on your fourth finger.

Hold the top chopstick as you would a pencil. Now practice moving the top chopstick to touch the bottom one. After you have practiced moving it back and forth for a while, now imagine picking up something. Remember, the bottom one never moves. Now try again eating your popcorn one piece at a time. Before long you'll be a pro.

Have you ever wondered …?

- How to eat an artichoke?
  With your fingers peel off each leaf and dip the soft end into the sauce or butter provided. Pull the leaf through your teeth to enjoy the edible portion. This sounds gross, doesn't it, but it's so good. Discard what is left of the leaf by putting it on the side of the plate and peel off the next leaf repeating the process until you discover the thistle portion. Scrape the thistle away and cut the heart of the artichoke into several pieces and eat them using your fork- not your fingers.

- Asparagus?
  In Europe, each piece of asparagus is eaten with the fingers but in the U.S.A. we cut it into pieces and eat it with a fork.

- Fried chicken?
  Use your knife and fork. Fried chicken is only eaten with the fingers casually with the family or at a picnic.

- Bones?
  If you are eating small birds or quail, squab, even frog legs the little bones may be delicately held in one hand and brought to your mouth. No slurping or gnawing allowed. Tiny bones from fish or bone slivers from fowl may find their way into your mouth. Just remove them with your thumb and index finger and place them on the side of your plate. If you do happen to swallow one, take a piece of bread and eat it quickly. It will coat the little bone and help you most often digest it without a problem.

- Tails on or off?
  Large shrimp are eaten in two bites and if possible cut with a fork. Shrimp with the tails left on may be held by the tail, dipped in sauce and eaten discarding the tail. Often, I cut off the tail portion and dip the shrimp in the sauce using a cocktail fork. You may do either and be correct.

- Bananas or plantains?
  When dining at a table, peel the fruit and eat it with a knife and fork. If you are eating a banana away from a table then peel the banana to the next bite-not the whole thing.

- Terms
  - Connoisseur – one with expert knowledge, of the arts and a person with discriminating taste
  - Epicurean – one who has excellent taste for food.
  - Gourmet – a good judge of food and drink. One who knows!

Remember: "You don't know what you don't know – but others do!" You have the keys.

# CAUTIONS

# The Risky Business of Travel

With so much business travel and family vacations being spent outside of our country, it can be risky business. Now is a good time to address the issue of security and give some serious thought to measures you should take to provide for your personal safety.

Unfortunately, the danger and threat of bodily harm exists everywhere these days. Our own country is no exception. When you are not a citizen of another country and travel within its borders, some precautions are best to be taken into consideration. Military and diplomatic personnel, along with major corporations, are briefed about security issues when the trip takes them abroad. For those business travelers and their families who do not have the opportunity to attend security briefings, the following information is important advice to consider for safety, when you are traveling alone or with others.

If you plan to remain in a city outside of the United States for much longer than 24 hours, the Department of State recommends you take the time to visit the U.S. Embassy and register. In case of an emergency, the Embassy will be able to locate you quickly if necessary. In addition, you also may be reached, without delay, if a dangerous situation exists which possibly would call for evacuation for health or security reasons.

Be alert, inconspicuous and try to keep a low profile. Forget the tourist wardrobe but rather dress conservatively so as not to appear either gullible or affluent. Travel light with a minimum of valuables. Women especially should leave their best jewelry at home.

Use travelers' checks and carry one or two credit cards instead of cash. Remember to take an extra set of passport photos and photocopy your passport information in case of loss or theft.

Book non-stop flights, if possible, and use covered luggage tags with the name of your business and business address only - not your home address and phone number. While on the plane or train, do not volunteer too much personal information to strangers.

When you travel through the city, stay away from alleyways, shortcuts and poorly lighted streets. Beware of pickpockets and take only officially marked taxis. Watch your alcohol intake and use only licensed tour guides even though you may get a bargain. You may get more than you bargained for instead.

Avoid public demonstrations and civil disturbances. If and when you see them taking place or, for that matter, any act of violence, leave the area immediately.

In your hotel or resort, always check with the front desk or the hotel concierge about safe areas and the best time to exercise. Don't just assume you can run or walk your usual two or three miles. When you do venture out, be sure to secure your passport and travelers' checks before you leave, carry a belt bag with some money, and the copy of your passport, a map and the name, address and phone number of your hotel.

If you are given a name badge by your company, a convention or conference, remove it before leaving the event or meeting. Do not wear your name badge as you walk through the hotel or in the elevator. It does nothing for your appearance and removing it is a definite security measure. Don't take luggage or t-shirts with your children's names printed on them if your children are included on your trip. Children should also dress conservatively.

Never answer your door without verifying who is there. If "room service" arrives and you haven't ordered any, don't open the door but call the front desk at once. Even if housekeeping knocks with fresh towels, tell them to leave them and you will get them later.

Finally, use good old common sense. When your intuition tells you not to do it, by all means don't. Enjoy your trip but remember that traveling outside of the United States without taking proper security precautions is risky business.

# Promotional Gift Giving

I thought I should visit a topic which spiked the blood pressure levels of some of my readers.

Printers, promotional item companies and those who create lovely gift baskets seemed to disagree with an article I wrote suggesting business gifts should not be imprinted with the giver's business logo. I stand by my opinion and want to address the issue more thoroughly.

Being a business person myself, I do understand marketing and the necessity to increase sales at every opportunity. Small businesses in particular have limited promotional funds and need to get the most bang for their buck. I also understand that business wants to be assured the recipients' of holiday gifts or those given for various reasons know and recognize from whom those thoughtful items were sent.

One of my reader's comments was "business should only give a gift if it will have a nice business impact. It is far less expensive, in bulk, to get a promotional item with your logo on it." This is not news to me, but herein lies the crux of the matter and our parting of the ways.

I believe that a company's excellent customer service policy, reflected constantly throughout the year, is more important than a gesture with business impact at holiday time.

Marketing and increased sales come from a company's professional presence and service in everything they do – from product quality to employee attitude and training. The flagrant use of in-your-face self and business promotion is not a gift.

A gift for the holidays or as a symbol of appreciation, or to mark a special occasion at anytime should not have a business logo on it. If it does it becomes a promotional item – perhaps a little larger and more elaborate than a trade-show give away.

That having been said, the box or wrapping the gift is in, certainly can be identified by the giver's logo or branding. There certainly would be no doubt as to who presented the gifts.

A lovely card, in good taste, accomplishes the same identification and if desired and time permits, it could contain a personal handwritten message which is certain to impress, is inexpensive and very sincere.

For those in the business of manufacturing or selling promotional items, printing or branding, I respect your profession and the need to market your products and services. Many promotional items make excellent holiday gift presentations. Printers can go crazy printing bags, containers and wraps with personalization, logos and greetings all over them.

To WOW your clients and impress them with your creativity or that of your team is a marketing tool in itself. Because you have received dozens of gifts with logos or business imprints on them doesn't make it right. With business to business gifts, the enclosure card or packaging should be identified by the name or company name of the giver.

If the gift itself is imprinted, stamped, engraved or etched, it should be with the recipients' name, company name or logo not the senders. In fact, it is a very nice gesture to give a personalized gift. But to place your own identification on the gift, even though your intention as an appreciative business person is well-placed, the item itself is no longer a gift but becomes a promotional item.

One idea that came from a very creative designer of gift baskets was shared with me. Her client, in the construction business, gave baskets she designed not in the usual wicker or card-board box but in bright red tool boxes filled with gourmet munchies.

Just think about it and how your team can create a gift which is unique and memorable. No logos on the tool boxes but labels galore could be placed on the paper packaging and the ribbon. Those tool boxes will no doubt be used in many different ways for years to come.

The recipient of your gift should not be compelled to nor have the responsibility of advertising for the gift giver.

Hold this thought. It is not about you but gift giving is all about how you are perceived and remembered for your thoughtfulness.

# Free Advice

Recently I was asked by a physician, "What do I do when an acquaintance wants to get answers to a medical question while attending a social event?" Of course, the doctor was doing the same thing with me, at the event we attended, by asking me for my advice pertaining to an etiquette question.

Sometimes we forget that when professionals are asked questions outside of the office, they never get paid for the consultation or advice. Medical doctors, in particular, rarely have enough information to make a proper diagnosis or make appropriate treatment recommendations while standing in the buffet line. People are often insistent and are disappointed when specific information is not given or questions are not answered because doctors are cornered or pressed into opinions without benefit of an examination or knowledge of medical history. This should not give cause for the person asking for information to feel rebuffed or that the professional is wrong for not dispensing the advice.

Without giving it much thought, most of us at one time or another have asked a professional for advice, an opinion, or direction on how, why, when and where. The professional could be a carpenter, plumber, electrician, veterinarian, lawyer or librarian. The type of profession is not the point. Asking for free advice is just something we should try to avoid. We need to make appointments, get estimates and approach professionals by respecting their area of expertise and their time.

That having been said, the medical community has a set of problems all its own which need to be addressed – some from the doctor's point of view and others from the patient's.

An example of a doctor's dilemma might be to meet a patient outside the office environment who they have seen, very personally, in various forms of undress or perhaps have operated on. The patient has placed his or her trust and faith in Doctor X and feels a personal connection, but the doctor can't remember the patient's name. Doctor X should not feel embarrassed, because this happens to everyone. If this situation applies to you, doctor or not, just go up to the person with your hand extended and say your name. You might also add, "It's nice to see you again." The person you have met will have to repeat his or her name after you have said yours and the conversation flows easily from there on.

Another question asked of me is how a doctor should introduce himself to a patient. In my opinion, the doctor most often wants the patient to be comfortable, trusting and confident. I suggest the doctor introduce himself without giving an honorific. For example, "Good morning, Mrs. Brown, I am Jack X, the hand surgeon you came to see today." Mrs. Brown will respond with respect by giving the doctor the honorific he deserves: "Good morning, Doctor X." By saying his first and last name, Doctor X has not given permission to call him Jack. Mrs. Brown will continue to address him as Doctor. His professional presence has not been diminished. One needs to command respect, not demand it.

A very stressful part of a doctor's job is to give a patient an unfortunate finding about his or her medical condition. Perhaps the news relates to a significant problem, cancer or an incurable disease. Sometimes there are no treatment options and the doctor, though uncomfortable having to deliver this message, must communicate this serious prognosis.

Even though the doctor experiences angst, it is always best to begin with a positive. It has been shown over and over that most people can accept anything negative if it begins with a positive comment and ends with a positive. I didn't say they would *like* it; I said they can *accept* it. The doctor must find ways to tell patients what they *can* do rather than what they can't, after the bad news is delivered. Simply saying they have to live with it is unacceptable. Their patients need to know *how* they can live with it.

One of the most adversarial situations for doctors is when a patient asks for additional pain medication and is refused because it is not warranted. Once again, the doctor's training and experience must be acknowledged and the patient should be reminded that the refusal is not personal but professional. The positive, negative, positive response to the patient's request will most often be accepted if the professional exhibits a caring, understanding attitude.

I don't know many people who are happy with the word "no." We must try to eliminate that word from our vocabulary as much as possible by saying the same thing in other ways. This takes practice.

On the other side of the coin, the patient's feelings also need to be acknowledged and respected by the physician.

The attitude of some physicians carries with it an elitist tone, which they think garners respect for their career choice and position. They forget that smiles beget smiles, kindness begets kindness, and being full of oneself or elitist begets disrespect because it is demeaning. A doctor should not appear egocentric. Doctors need to be aware of their facial expressions. I know doctors who wear the "doctor face" even when telling patients good news or meeting them for the first time. Smiling is one thing that is contagious, and we don't mind catching it.

Most patients complain if their physician does not give them enough time to discuss their physical (sometimes emotional) problem. They also complain if they are kept waiting too long after their appointment time. Both of these situations can be helped by a thoughtful, well-trained receptionist who has a modicum of good communication skills. One scenario that comes to mind is when a doctor was called away for an emergency and a patient was not notified and still in the waiting room when the receptionist turned out the lights. Doctors, please get your receptionists some training. You don't need your patient's blood pressure to rise in the waiting room.

Doctors are technically educated to the max, but they also are in business. It appears that most do not have a clue about how to run an office. If they are going to be in practice, they are in business and should take an extra course in business etiquette. Some doctors dress so casually, they actually appear sloppy. Just because they have years of technical training in their profession, that doesn't give them *carte blanche* to dress unprofessionally or run a disorganized office.

Business dictates that phone calls should be returned. If a doctor has an emergency or cannot for any reason return a patient's phone call, then someone should be appointed to do so. To be ignored by the physician's office personnel is to be diminished, and to be diminished is devastating.

Some doctors' offices are beautifully appointed and maintained. Even doctors in very high positions should take an interest in the appearance of their offices and exam rooms. A coat of paint does wonders, and stacks of files on the floor don't do much for a patient's confidence. Bunny rabbits and stuffed bears on the reception desk along with drink containers, pictures and notes taped all around don't speak highly of a professional image.

Respect should be shown to physicians and also to patients and their families. Stress is not an excuse because it, too, works both ways. Consideration of time and space are necessary in any profession. Some doctors should be congratulated for going the extra mile to make certain their image and communication reflect their executive presence. Others should take note and raise the bar, following through on their professional image of the training and expertise they have worked so hard to achieve. As in any profession, excellent communication is key, both oral and visual.

# International Perceptions
# and Misconceptions

E ven when your voice is still you are communicating. Unspoken language is just as important when you are conducting business in other countries as it is here in the United States.

Communication varies in "high-context" and "low-context" cultures. High-context (HC) communication relies mainly on relationships for information. Lifelong friends often use HC or implicit messages which are nearly impossible for an outsider to understand. In a high-context culture, not disclosing something is viewed as sneaky or mysterious even though they depend on non-verbal communications.

High context cultures rely on role identity interaction and their words have exact meanings. They have many rituals they follow and operate or polychromic time. This means there are several things happening at once. You may recognize some of these traits in friends and associates from Japan, China, Korea, Spain, Greece, Turkey, the Arab countries, Latin America, Eastern Asia and the Southern and Eastern Mediterranean.

You will find this HC culture to be highly distractible, they change plans easily and are almost never on time. They are loyal to their friends and build life long relationships.

Diverse backgrounds and cultures cause us to be judged or viewed in a different way in several countries. What might be acceptable in one might be offensive in another, and the reaction to subtle differences will often escalate and could lead to aggression.

Low-Context cultures (LC) such as Switzerland, Germany, Canada, the U.S. and Scandinavia are more segmented and linear. Appointments and schedules are considered important because time is a commodity and promptness is emphasized. Low Context cultures are generally monochromic and tend to do one thing at a time.

They follow plans, get involved with a project and concentrate on it. Low Content cultures follow rules of privacy and consideration and have great respect for private property. Even though they deal with short-term relationships, they are fairly well informed. Excessive talking is viewed as belaboring the obvious and redundant.

You may wonder why I bring up High Context and Low Context cultures and polychromic and monochromic time, when they don't really affect your day to day business dialog or appointment schedule. Be prepared. Knowing how to shake hands with those from other countries isn't enough today. You may not be dealing internationally in your business but thousands of business people across our land are taking the leap into the global market. I have often said, "Prior planning prevents poor performance" and this is just the beginning of a myriad of information intended to share with you regarding the protocols of international communication. If you make an effort to learn and adopt the cultural traditions and nuances of the countries with which you intend to do business, you have a much better chance for success.

It is very easy for HC and LC cultures to fail to recognize these basic differences in behavior and communication.

Be prepared.

# FINALLY

# Our Flag

With the attack on America stirring our hearts and awakening our sense of patriotism, this may be the time to review or bring to your attention, the protocols needed to ensure proper respect for our Stars and Stripes.

- The flag of these United States should be raised and lowered by hand. It should be unfurled then hoisted quickly to the top of the staff. Lower it with dignity. Place no objects over the flag.
- The flag should be displayed only from sunrise to sunset. If the flag is to be displayed after sunset, it must have a floodlight or spotlight focused on it.
- After a death, the flag is flown at half-mast. It is known that as early as 1627, this was a sign of mourning. It has been continued to the present day.
- If our flag is to be flown at half-mast, it should be hoisted to the peak for an instant, and then lowered to half-mast.
- On Memorial Day, display it at half-mast only until noon, and then hoist it to the top of the staff.
- Take every precaution to prevent the flag from becoming soiled or allowed to touch the ground or floor. It should not be displayed in stormy weather or on extremely windy days and should never be folded if it is wet.
- When the flag is raised or lowered, or passing in review, or in a parade, those men and women present in uniform should render the right hand salute. When not in uniform, men

should always remove their hats or caps and place them at the left shoulder, the hand being over the heart. Women should place the right hand over the heart.

- Never use the flag as drapery of any sort, or place anything on it such as a letter, figure, design or picture.
- When carried, it should be aloft and free with no other flag flown or carried above our Stars and Stripes except the United Nations flag at the U.N. Headquarters.
- The print of honor for the American Flag is on the extreme left, from the point of the observer. As business people we must remember at a meeting or dinner, the flag should be at the speaker's right or the observer's left.
- When flags of two or more nations are displayed, they should be on separate staffs, of the same height and the flags should be of equal size. International usage forbids the display of one nation above that of another in the time of peace. If it is not possible to display two or more flags at the same height, it is not proper protocol to display them together at all.
- When our flag is displayed over the middle of the street, it should be suspended vertically with the union to the north on an east and west street, or to the east on a north and south street.
- When flags of states, cities or societies are flown with our national flag, the U.S. flag should always be at the center and at the peak.
- At times when the flag is used to cover a casket, it should be placed with the union, also know as the canton, at the head and over the left shoulder. The flag should never be lowered into the grave or allowed to touch the ground.
- When displayed flat whether indoors or out, either horizontally or vertically against a wall or window, the union should be upper most to the flag's right. That is to the observer's left.

There are a few more protocols listed in the Flag Etiquette chapter of my book, *Bound for the Boardroom*, but these are enough to get you through the basics. Our many Veterans are aware of these rules and as I've said so many times, "You don't know what you don't know, but others do."

Even with help from other countries, our forefathers fought and died for our freedoms. Others today, around the world are fighting and dying for theirs. The love and appreciation we feel for our country and the pride in our citizens, living and passed, with each contribution made along their way, is made evident by the manner in which we display our national flag on our business property., our homes or on parade. Let's do it with respect and solemn thoughts of thanksgiving for the sacrifices made on our behalf.

I am so proud, blessed and grateful to be an American citizen. To all the veterans who have made it possible for our flag to fly free. Thank You! Thank You! Thank You!

# Dates to Fly the U.S. Flag

This is a complete list of dates throughout the year on which you should fly our U.S. flag. On all days, the flag should be raised to and flown full staff unless otherwise specified.

New Year's Day – January 1
Martin Luther King Day – third Monday in January
Inauguration Day – January 20 every fourth year
Lincoln's Birthday – February 12
Presidents Day – third Monday in February
Washington's Birthday – February 22
Army Day – April 6
V-E Day – May 8
Armed Forces Day – third Saturday in May
Memorial Day – forth Monday in May
Flag Day – June 14
Independence Day – July 4
V-J Day – August 10
Labor Day – first Monday in September
Patriot Day – September 11 (half-staff)
Constitution Day – September 17
Columbus Day – second Monday in October
United Nations Day – October 24
Navy Day – October 27
Elections Day – 2nd Tuesday in November (every 4th year)
Veterans Day – November 11
Thanksgiving – fourth Thursday in November
Pearl Harbor Day – December 7 (half-staff)
Christmas Day – December 25

# About the Author

Barbara B. Bergstrom is Executive Director of *Greetings: Voice – Image – Communications,* a leading etiquette and protocol company with offices in Chicago and Orlando. Her syndicated weekly column, "Executive Etiquette," appears in business publications across the country. Her book *Bound for the Boardroom* and its Spanish translation, *Rumbo al Éxito Empresarial,* have been adopted as "must have" management primers and favorites for corporate training and gift-giving.

A recognized authority on executive presence and international protocol, Barbara has an extensive list of clients that includes corporate, charitable, financial, governmental, hospitality, educational and medical organizations, as well as celebrities and entertainers. She is regularly featured on television and radio talk shows, where her dynamic wit and wisdom delight hosts and resonate with audiences. She is a gifted motivational speaker, and her customized seminars are widely attended nationally, and highly rated for content, humor and energy.

Barbara was educated in private preparatory schools in Chicago and attended the University of Texas, where she majored in mass communications. Following certification by the nation's most prestigious etiquette and protocol school, in Washington, D.C., she established the International Association of Independent Etiquette and Protocol Consultants. Barbara recently served as Vice President and Chief Protocol Officer of the International Council of Central Florida, under the auspices of the U.S. Secretary of State.

An accomplished presenter and public speaking coach, Barbara is a three-time Distinguished Toastmaster who received the "Toastmaster of the Year" award for the State of Florida and the Bahamas. She is also Protocol Officer for the international organization's Southeast region, which includes Florida, Alabama, Mississippi, Georgia, Louisiana, Texas, North Carolina, South Carolina, Virginia and the islands of the Bahamas.

# *Afterword*

Thank you to the United States Department of State for sharing some of the important information regarding the correct protocols found in this book.

Visit Barbara B. Bergstrom on the Web at
www.greetings-eps.com

E-mail: greetingseps@aol.com
Fax: (407) 292-0306
Mailing address: P.O. Box 617554, Orlando, FL 32835

You may contact Barbara for information regarding her availability for speaking engagements, private sessions, customized in-house training seminars or print articles. Her information-packed programs are problem-solving, educational, motivational, professional, energetic and uncomplicated. The results are immediate!

Barbara's books include *Bound for the Boardroom,* an easy-to-read guide to professional presence, and the Spanish version, *Rumbo al Éxito Empresarial,* along with *Don't Forget Your Keys,* and are available on her Web site, at Barnes & Noble and at Amazon.com in hard cover, softcover and e-book formats. Watch for Barbara's next book, *Thanks for having me"…. and other funny foibles.*